Apples, etc.

(overleaf) **Home Environment**, 1968. Ceramic, acrylic paint, polyester resin, metal, silkscreen 65.5 × 39.0 × 52.5 cm.
14 Rotten Apples, 1970. Ceramic, glaze, Plexiglas base, 19.1 × 28.0 × 25.0 cm.

30 Grapefruit, 1970. Ceramic, glaze, Plexiglas base, 32.0 × 49.5 × 49.5 cm.

Blue Running Shoes, c. 1973. Earthenware, glaze, wood, glass, paint, 101.5 × 105.4 × 16.1 cm.

Picnic with Clock and Bird, 1976. Ceramic, acrylic paint, varnish, 22.0 × 29.0 × 23.0 cm.

Piece of Water: Libya, 1981. Oil on canvas, 197.5 × 167.0 cm.

GATHIE FALK

WITH ROBIN LAURENCE

Apples, etc.

AN ARTIST'S MEMOIR

Figure.1
Vancouver / Berkeley

for Elizabeth

CONTENTS

Gathie Falk, 2016

INTRODUCTION
(BEFORE)

THERE WAS A TIME, long ago, when I thought I would like nothing more than to be a street-corner musician. What I became, and have been for many years, is an artist. Not a singer, not a pianist, not a violinist, but a visual artist.

My apprenticeship was a long one. I was born, in the little sheep town of Alexander, Manitoba, on January 31, 1928, two years after my Mennonite parents fled to Canada from Russia. My father died when I was ten months old and my brothers were nine and three. After that, our lives were marked by poverty and frequent moves from place to place, and we often depended upon the charity of others. But I was a maker from the earliest days.

I remember sitting on a windowsill when I was about two, holding a pair of scissors, saying "scissors" out loud and triumphantly. I learned how to put them to good use. I cut a hole in a piece of cloth and tied a string around the waist to make a doll dress. Family and friends said, "Oh, she's going to be a seam-stress," which disturbed me. That was never my ambition. Still, when I was in my teens, I designed my own dresses, which my mother sewed for me, and later, I made my dresses myself. Later still, I earned my living sewing, not dresses but pockets for suitcases.

From a very young age, I wanted to know how to draw, and I thought my elders could show me the way. When I was about three, I insisted that my mother should draw me a picture. This was during a period when I was being treated for eczema. There were no doctors in our rural Mennonite community; my mother, like others there, relied on home remedies. The one used on my eczema was a mixture of cow dung, mud, and tar, applied every evening after dinner. It stank and it burned and I'm sure I com-plained bitterly, but on it went. I remember that I sat on my moth-er's well-protected lap during the treatment—and we were not a lap-sitting family—until it dried. After I had endured this foul mixture and been washed clean, I could sit in her lap again while she told me a story, the same story about a baby duck, lost and then found again, over and over, much to my brothers' disgust.

One evening I asked her to draw me a picture of a woman, a mama. She said no. I kept saying, "Draw me a picture," and she kept saying no, until she eventually relented. She somehow pro-cured a pencil and a sheet of paper and, holding the pencil in her fist, she drew a series of strong vertical lines. I can still see those pencil marks, up and down, up and down, no bulges, no curves.

"There," she said.

I objected. "No!"

"What?" she asked.

"A head!" She put a tiny head at the top. "And feet," I said.

She did that and said, "There! Finished!"

I demanded arms. She drew long loose arms waving on each side of the body and again said, "Finished!"

I protested. "Chickens!"

She drew chickens, and then declared, "That's the last drawing I will ever make for you!"

I asked why and she said, "Because I can't draw." And that was true.

In those early days, there were no materials for making art in our home, no crayons or coloured pencils or paint. The only paper we had was kept on a high shelf and used for letters. During the brief period of my mother's second marriage, I was given a set of watercolours for Christmas. I didn't know what to do with them. I wanted perfection, but I couldn't control the sloppy wet marks I made.

I don't remember exactly when my drawing tools and I came together in a satisfactory way. It might have been when I was at school in Winnipeg, in grade two. I was obsessed with drawing heads, but they were a source of worry to me. They didn't look right. For a time I did as the other children in my class did, tracing a circle around the top of a paste bottle, then adding a couple of dots and a semicircle—eyes and mouth. It seemed like a simple solution to my drawing problem, but I was not really happy with those unnaturally round and simple heads either.

At home one day, I asked my brother Jack to draw a head. He was, after all, much older than I was. Surely he knew how. He took on the assignment and worked seriously, drawing and erasing and drawing again and erasing again to get it right. He handed his effort over with some satisfaction but, to my horror, it looked awful. I said so. "Well then," he told me with some annoyance, "draw your own heads."

Eventually, I did. By grade four or five, I was repeatedly drawing two fantasy pictures. The first was of a glamorous woman in a long dress with an upswept hairdo and a fur stole. The other was of a girl's playroom loaded with dolls, dozens of dolls, and all the other toys I wished I had—a doll carriage, a dollhouse, doll clothes.

One day, my teacher, the dreaded Miss Vanderhoek who had once strapped me for being late, took my drawings away from me. With a sarcastic "Look what she's been doing!" she put them up on the chalkboard for all to see. I think her intention was to embarrass me because I had been drawing in class instead of reading my geography book, but it was also a mark of distinction. I felt humiliation and pride—definitely a mixed experience. I knew she admired my drawings because a few years after that, when I was thirteen, she recommended me to take part in Saturday-morning art classes in downtown Winnipeg. This was a privilege granted to just a few of the most talented kids in each school.

The art lessons were also a mixed experience. I didn't always have the money for transit fare there and back, five cents each way. The classes, which were big, were in a civic building on Vaughan Street that had a museum in the basement, an auditorium on the main floor, and an art gallery on the top floor. My brother Gordon and I had sometimes slipped into the museum and art gallery on our unsupervised expeditions downtown, but my memory is that the gallery was always unlit when we were there. If we stayed long enough, images might coalesce out of the darkness.

The first art lessons I attended were in the basement museum, sitting on the floor, drawing the stuffed animals in their glass cases. This was my first experience of drawing from life—if you could call taxidermic animals "life." Previously I had created images out of my imagination or copied photographs in magazines. My work was typical of a child's first efforts at depicting the unfamiliar: a tiny creature stranded in the middle of a large piece of paper. The instructors said, "Bigger, bigger, bigger!" It was a very fearful exercise.

Later we were promoted to a less frightening area of the building, but I was depressed because all the other children drew and painted better than I did. They took instructions better too. I was told to use colours that made no sense to me. I was stubborn in my convictions about how things looked and should be represented. After a year or so, we had a few art history classes, during which the instructors showed us reproductions of Impressionist and Post-Impressionist paintings. When they brought out a picture of a vivid reddish-orange dog painted by Paul Gauguin, I decided that I had had enough of this school. Like most young teenagers at the time, I was a realist. Dogs weren't orange! I took my pastels and went home. I didn't go back.

Music filled the creative void. I had always loved singing and wished I could have lessons like a girl I knew who sang up and down the scales better than any bird. I had a strong voice, but not a trained one. I couldn't sing the high notes. I also wanted to play piano and took every opportunity to get my hands on an organ owned by the family of my friend Helen Fast, and the piano of other friends, the Wittenbergs. I got no further than "Chopsticks." Still, singing came naturally, and I made a splash one Christmas Eve when our Sunday school class performed the last song on the program, "Lo, How a Rose E'er Blooming." We had been tutored to sing in two-part harmony by the choirmaster, Mr. Wiebe. It seems that my voice rang out above the others: I enjoyed acclaim and was asked to sing in the church choir, a great honour at the age of fifteen.

Because of this small success, friends of my mother's persuaded her that I should have singing lessons. Victor Friesen, our local music man, was engaged for the project. When I was a child, I would hear him walking along the road, singing at the top of his voice, just walking and singing classical music and hymns. It was wonderful. We came to a practical agreement: I would babysit his three children, and he would teach me to sing. At home, between lessons, I would practise, picking out the notes on a guitar and learning new songs—German lieder and other classical compositions for the voice. And then another little miracle happened: an anonymous donor, someone whose name I never learned, offered to pay Mr. Friesen to give me conducting and music theory lessons. I was fully immersed in my new musical life. Then my promising existence came to a crashing halt.

In my mid-teens, after completing grade nine, I had to drop out of school. My family still owed money to Canadian Pacific Ships for the steamship passage that had brought them as immigrants to Canada from Russia. The company had suspended its demands for repayment during the Depression, but afterwards, when most people were doing better, it tracked us down and pounced. By that time, my brothers had both left home; Jack was married and Gordon was engaged. My mother was sickly and had never learned English. The burden of repayment fell to me. While going to school, I had worked part-time picking strawberries, cleaning house, babysitting. But now I had to find a full-time job.

For the first summer, I looked after a three-year-old girl. The child was naughty, the work was mind numbing, and there was little money in it. Then I found a job in a Macdonalds Consolidated warehouse, filling cellophane bags with raisins, dates, brown sugar, peas, beans, and chocolate rosebuds to be sold in Safeway stores. A lot of women shared this work, and they also shared stories about themselves and what they'd done on the weekend. When the others discovered I was taking voice lessons, they asked me to sing for them. I did, and they quickly closed all the windows because my voice was so loud. Together we sang all the popular songs of the day, including the war songs that promised love and laughter and peace ever after. The singing helped alleviate the boredom of standing in front of big metal tubs mounted on long trestle tables, filling bags, weighing them, then folding, stapling, and packing them into wooden crates.

My teachers deplored the fact that I was dropping out of school—and I did too. I minded the menial work much less than having my education cut short. I was a very good student, I loved learning, and, naturally, I wanted a bright future for myself. Leaving school caused me immense distress. However, during the second year of my warehouse work, I discovered that I could finish high school by correspondence. This meant that I had to stop my music lessons but not singing in the choir. By then I had made my way through the music theory book and was also able to conduct small singing groups. Still, it was a tough grind, working full-time, studying at night and on weekends, and attending choir rehearsals.

Since I had no stories to tell the other women, and I didn't like the tobacco smoke that hung heavily in the lunchroom, I sat in a nook and pored over my textbooks and school assignments during our breaks. This standoffishness did not make me popular, but I often redeemed myself by making the others laugh. Once, when I had been sitting on a crate for far too long, one of the girls said indignantly, "Gathie, how come you're still sitting there? You're being very selfish—you should be ashamed of yourself." I paused and then said, "Yes, I am ashamed of myself." That brought a loud laugh. I got up to do the next job.

By June 1946, I had repaid the CP debt and written all my grade ten exams, passing with the highest marks in the province. This was the end of my life in Winnipeg. At eighteen, I moved with my mother, brother Gordon, and sister-in-law Edith to the golden land of British Columbia. Jack and his wife, Vera, were living in Vancouver, and my mother had cousins who lived in the Fraser Valley and spoke glowingly of it. Mother always had a dream of living again in the country, on a little farm with a cow and chickens, making bricks, drying them in the sun, building our own house. For a while this dream appealed to me too. It didn't happen.

Gordon and Edith settled in Vancouver, and we stayed for a while in Yarrow with Mother's cousins, the Brauns, sleeping in their living room. Then we moved into a room in the house next door. I worked picking raspberries in a huge field and plucked chickens in a smelly processing plant. The work and the pay were wretched, and we moved again, to Chilliwack, where I got a waitressing job in a hotel. We looked neat and colourful in our uniforms, fresh every day, with equally fresh aprons. I was told to wear lipstick, which I did, putting it on when I got to the hotel and removing it before I got home. I didn't want to offend my mother. I learned how to fold a napkin and carry three plates at a time, but I was a terrible waitress. My mind wasn't in it. I couldn't remember orders; I couldn't remember which table had ordered what dishes. I felt like an idiot, a belief audibly shared by a number of customers. My regulars, mostly salesmen, got used to seeing me walk with great speed and determination out of the kitchen, then stop suddenly, turn, and go back to retrieve my forgotten order. They would laugh heartily. Eventually I got things done, but there was an awful lot of back-and-forthing.

When I arrived at the hotel, I was the lowest person on the ladder. After eight months, near the end of my stint there, I was at the top because all the other waitresses had left. That was truly scary because it meant I would be in charge. I didn't know how to run things. The community didn't really suit my mother and me, either. The church was too far away and too difficult to get to, my waitressing schedule meant that I sometimes had to work Sundays, the rest of the family was in Vancouver, and I needed a better job.

In the spring of 1947, my mother and I moved again, zooming like homing pigeons to Vancouver. I realized that I loved cities: I loved having access to a big library and to all the other amenities of urban life. We rented two rooms in a house on 25th Avenue, near Fraser Street, and found a church we could easily walk or bus to. With the church and its choir, we had the gifts of friends and a community. I went job-hunting at once, and there's a dull grey photo of me, taken by a street photographer downtown. I am wearing a raincoat and babushka, and my expression is grim. Very grim. I was heading out from the government employment agency to my first job in Vancouver, in a luggage factory.

My task there was to sew pockets for the inside of suitcases. The pockets were elasticized at the top, the fabric was cut at an angle, across the grain, and it was very hard to feed the elastic and the cloth into the sewing machine at the same time. Although I had sewn many of my own clothes at home in Winnipeg, I wasn't used to operating a power sewing machine. It seemed as if I broke hundreds of needles. The foreman, Jim, was very kind, very tolerant. He stood near me, one arm wrapped around his waist, leaning on the elbow of the other arm, with his face in his hand. As soon as the needle broke, he put in a new one. Eventually I mastered the machine and earned the nickname Speed.

I was very grateful to Jim for his long-suffering care. We became good friends, and when he suggested I move to another luggage factory where he would be the new foreman, I followed him there. It was a good job for a while, but we had come from a unionized shop to a place that wasn't—and that didn't raise anyone's wages. To my dismay, the men were paid more than the women. When I took up this issue with the boss, a fine person, he said men should be paid more because they had families to support. I said that I had to support my mother. His response was to offer my mother a job as a domestic worker in his household. I cried. I could not explain that my mother was fragile, mentally and physically. That she couldn't speak English. That she would never be able to work for a stranger. I just cried.

The luggage factory work took dexterity but, again, it was terribly boring. Still, my life was crammed full. I had resumed high school correspondence courses, and each day I would ride my bicycle to work, study during my lunch periods, read a book as a treat during my coffee breaks, go home, have my dinner, study some more, and go to bed. Somewhere in there, I also took music lessons, sang in two choirs, and practised my violin.

The violin was a gift from my mother, and it was my first Christmas present in Vancouver. It was an old instrument found by my brother Jack in a second-hand shop on Main Street, but it served its purpose. In January 1948, I began violin lessons with Walter Neufeld and music theory lessons with his brother, Menno. After studying for six months, I played the grade one violin exam and got first-class marks. I jumped to grade five violin the next year and did not get first-class marks. In my third year of lessons, I barely passed the grade six exams.

It became clear that I had hit a wall. I was not going to be an accomplished violinist, not even a street-corner musician. I developed severe, debilitating pain in my arm and shoulder, and I could hardly lift a cup, never mind do my work or play the violin. It might have been neuritis or some form of repetitive strain injury, but it seems to me now that there was a strong psychological component to this pain. I was sick and tired of working in a luggage factory. I couldn't continue with the violin. I was completely flattened.

My mother and Walter could see how depressed and discouraged I was and decided I should become a schoolteacher. I was furious at them both for making this decision for me. I never, ever wanted to be a teacher. I had a vision of myself walking up and down the aisle by the windows, dictating spelling words to the kids. That image was unspeakably dreary.

Earlier, during a music lesson, Walter had asked me, "What would you really like to do?" The next week, after much thought, I said, "I would like to be an artist." Not much came of Walter's question and my answer, at least not then. But there it was. I wanted to be an artist.

MY
EDUCATION
(LEARNING,
TEACHING,
DOING)

IN 1952, AT THE AGE of twenty-four, I enrolled in a one-year teaching certificate program at the Provincial Normal School in Vancouver. I did it unwillingly, gritting my teeth, not realizing that teaching would open the door for me—the door to being an artist.

At the time, I had been supporting my mother for eight years; it seemed only fair that I could ask my brothers to look after her while I was a student. I rented a room near the Normal School, and my mother stayed with Jack and Gordon, first with one, then the other. I continued to work evenings at the luggage factory, and after being laid off there, I cleaned houses on Saturdays. And then it turned out that my brothers and their wives couldn't live with my mother. She was too bossy, in the kitchen and elsewhere. They shipped her back to me, and we moved into a slightly larger rented room, a turn of events I very much resented. I had had only a few

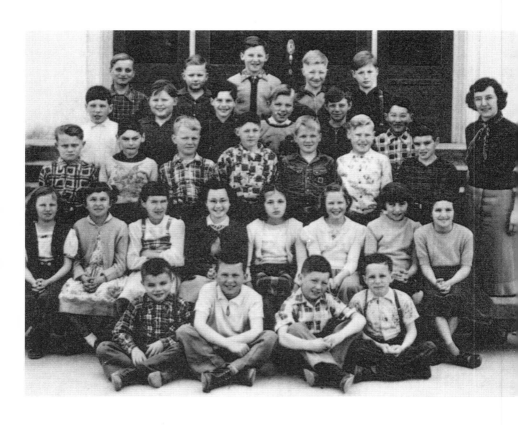

A class photo with my first elementary
school students, Surrey, 1953. After a rough
start, I learned how to be a good teacher.

months of living by myself and loved it. Then I was forced to share my space and be responsible for my mother again. Our landlord, who lived in the basement, added to the discomfort by playing shortwave radio until two or three in the morning. The transmissions were loud, quiet, loud, squeal-y, and I couldn't sleep.

Despite these difficulties, important changes were taking place within me. While I was waiting for a bus on Cambie Street, I noticed some reproductions of Gauguin paintings in a shop window. And I remembered the orange dog that had so annoyed my teenage self in Winnipeg. Suddenly the colour made sense. I could see what a wonderful painting it was, what a treasure. Gauguin's orange dogs, blue trees, red fields—all were precious and remarkable things.

I had continued drawing through my teens and after we arrived in Vancouver. And I had tried and failed to find an art teacher early on, while I was working at the luggage factory. I had no idea where the art school was—or even that one existed. But at Normal School I began to draw again with renewed energy and conviction. Our program included not only learning how to teach primary school but also refresher courses in history, geography, math, science, art, and music. My fellow students admired my drawings. The art teacher, however, was cold. He knew, as I now know, that drawing is not the most telling factor in an art career. You can draw with great facility and never become an artist. It's tenacity that matters.

My first teaching position in Surrey paid $1,800 a year, which was less than I had been earning at the luggage factory and a meagre income for me and my mother, whom I was still supporting. That was a disappointment. I didn't seem to have much of a natural talent for teaching either, and I had problems maintaining discipline in the classroom. During one of my student-teaching assignments, the supervising teacher took me aside and suggested that I try another profession. At that point, though, I couldn't see what else I might do to earn a living. There were few professions I could qualify for in the space of a year. I wasn't happy living in Surrey, which was then very rural. I missed the bright lights and busy sidewalks of Vancouver. The school was overcrowded, the teachers had to share classrooms and work in shifts, and the kids were rambunctious.

I left the Surrey job after a year, resigning before I could be fired. My principal thought I was a very good teacher. He was proud of all the art the students had produced under my guidance, but the district school inspector had another opinion of my educative abilities. He arrived in the classroom one day and demanded to see the children's exercise books. I had never once looked at them, and they were horrible—they were actually horrible looking. It was hard to believe I had assigned the exercises in these books, but I hadn't supervised or marked them. I had no idea how to teach when I first started. An additional sin in the inspector's eyes was that while he was in the classroom, I had permitted one of my students to stand on a desk to affix a classroom decoration high on the blackboard.

Adding to that ignominious end to my first year of teaching, my mother, who was in charge of our finances, cashed my last paycheque and lost the money. That was the money we were to live on for the next two months. Instead of going to teacher training in Victoria as my colleagues did, I spent the summer waitressing, housecleaning, and sorting fruit in a canning factory.

In the fall of 1954, however, I secured a job at Douglas Road Elementary School in Burnaby, a position I held until 1965. I learned how to be a fine teacher, especially of art, music, and literature. And I made good use of my years of musical training, conducting student choirs and teaching children how to sing. There was no child after grade three who was allowed to moan on and on, holding one sorry note. I would work with the whole class, saying, "Start down here, low like this, and then go up high like a fire engine, as high as you can." If you do that every day, the moaning one-note kid is going to find his voice. In my last year of teaching I had no choir, but every child in my two grade-seven classes could carry a tune.

The payoff for my years of teaching is that every now and then I meet someone I taught long ago. Two of my former students have become writers; another plays in a band. Another, still, approached me at an exhibition opening with a photograph of one of my first big choirs that was taken when she sang in it. She said choral singing was the most important thing in her life. At the opening of a retrospective exhibition in Vancouver a couple of years ago, a group of five women came up to me and were very sweet and congratulatory. They told me I had been their favourite teacher. What could be more gratifying? No suitcases have come back to talk to me, and not one Safeway bag filled with beans.

After my second year of teaching, I began to take summer courses in English, history, and German, towards a bachelor's degree in education. I also spent two summers in Victoria studying design, drawing, and painting with the artist Bill West. Afterwards, I started taking fine arts and art history courses at the University of British Columbia. Over the next few years, through both summer courses and evening classes, I studied with Lawren Harris Jr., J.A.S. (Jim) MacDonald, Jacques de Tonnancour, Audrey Capel Doray, Bill and David Mayrs, and Ron Stonier. Of them all, Jim MacDonald was the most influential for me, and the most supportive. He taught painting and drawing, but mostly he just gave us assignments, and then he would stand behind each student and gently critique his or her work. When he came to mine, he would say something like "Everything's melting to the left there" or "Everything's taking off and going into orbit over there." That would tell me the balance in my painting was wrong, something I initially couldn't see for myself. He always liked my work and was very sympathetic to what I was trying to achieve.

Naturally I fell in love with him. It was a chaste and honourable love, though. He was married.

Despite the times, I was more interested in German Expressionism, which was figurative, than in American Abstract Expressionism. I felt drawn to create a concrete image that was recognizable even though it might be distorted—and some of my imagery was very distorted. I wasn't interested in painting pretty pictures; I wanted to paint strong works. I also took two years of evening painting classes from Roy Oxlade, an art tough from England. In class, he insisted on total abstraction, whether you were working from a figure or a landscape. And he wouldn't let you use any bright colours, only tans, browns, greys, black, and white. This was an exercise in gesture and tonality, but it was also gruelling and exasperating. Somehow you had to generate a visual climax out of a sea of mud. You would paint with determination all evening, and Roy would look at your work and say, "That's shit" and walk away. Despite his harsh criticism, I learned a great deal from him. He taught me how to make a broad and meaningful brushstroke.

In 1962, I had the sudden understanding that my apprenticeship in painting was over. I was in a night class at the Vancouver School of Art and realized that I didn't want anyone standing behind me anymore, telling me what to paint or how. After that, I had the confidence to work on my own. I knew what I wanted to do.

I began exhibiting my paintings in group shows at the Vancouver Art Gallery, although I sold only one work at the time, and that was to a friend. It was probably ten years before I sold another painting. My expressionist works were not in vogue in the early 1960s. It was an age of Hard-Edge, Op, and Pop Art, with thin, flat paint application intended to look as if it had been laid on by a machine. I'd done enough factory work in my life. I wasn't interested in mimicking a machine.

By 1964, I had shifted degree programs to fine arts in education. I needed more art credits, and having exhausted all the painting and drawing courses at UBC, I began studying ceramics with Glenn Lewis. Glenn had apprenticed with the great British potter Bernard Leach in Cornwall and had also worked with the noted Canadian potter John Reeve in Devonshire. In the first year of studying with him, I made a lot of pots, and most of them I tossed into the bin. The classes were about learning, not making an object we could hold onto or give away as a Christmas present. By the end of the year, we had progressed enough that we were each allowed to keep a couple of our pots. Glenn kept one of mine, by the way.

Glenn also introduced us to ceramic sculpture, a discipline that initially puzzled me. I had once told Jim MacDonald that I didn't know how to look at abstract sculpture because I didn't know where it ended. "There's no frame," I said. On assignment I made a miniature tree, with individual leaves that could be hooked onto the branches. That idea must have lodged somewhere inside me because I can see it in the life-size papier mâché sculpture *Winter Tree with Leaves* that I created decades later. It is bare and bony and stands in my living room with a low square bed of gravel at its base. When I first exhibited *Winter Tree*, the installation included acrylic paintings of much-enlarged autumn leaves, not dangling from its branches but mounted on the walls around it.

Glenn was a wonderful teacher. He tried to turn us students into more thinking people—and that included thinking about the art of daily living. He was opening us up to an awareness of the forms and rituals of everyday life, and through the years these rituals—food prepared, meals shared, birthdays and holidays celebrated—have become an important part of my relationship with friends. Glenn also spoke about a life less driven by consumption and materialism, advocating voluntary simplicity before that term had been invented. If someone came into the classroom with an item she'd bought in a thrift store, he would exclaim about it and say, "Wow, that's a beautiful green woollen scarf, and look how long it is!" Initially I thought, "Hmmph, it's just an old scarf." For many years I had lived frugally out of necessity, not choice, and by then I was enjoying the modest material comforts that teaching allowed me. I could afford to buy a good new scarf if I wanted. But the lesson lingered, and later, after I had quit teaching, I started going to thrift stores and buying my clothes there too.

In 1965, during my second year studying with Glenn, I made a seven-foot ceramic sculpture titled *The General Explaining Why He Had To Use Napalm*, which stood for a few months in front of the education building at the University of British Columbia. The work was composed of a series of ceramic cylinders, mounted over and supported by a tall, upright pole. At the top was the general, about two feet high, with a flat head, a narrow face, and a wide mouth, open and twisted. As a Mennonite, I am a pacifist, but I didn't like anti-war demonstrations. I hated all that standing around; it seemed like a waste of time. I had too much energy. I was too driven to make things, to accomplish things. That sculpture, which is one of the few political works I've ever created, expressed my dismay at and opposition to the war in Vietnam. While making it, I experimented with individual ceramic shapes—a leg, shoes, boots, a suit coat—which, although not fully realized then, seeded ideas in my mind for future artworks.

That summer I started a commercial pottery with a fellow student, Charmian Johnson. She would go on to become an outstanding ceramicist whose work is keenly sought after by collectors. At first we threw pots at her place because she had a kick wheel, and we fired them in my electric kiln. The next summer I drew plans for a walk-in, high-fire gas kiln, which I was able to realize with a short-term grant from the Canada Council. Working with Charmian, and with help and advice from the ceramicist and teacher Tam Irving and others, we built the kiln in my garage. Wondrously, it passed inspection at City Hall. We fired a lot of pots, and I sold mine at a shop near Stanley Park. I can see my mother, standing in the hall with her hands on her hips, saying, "So you think you're going to make money with this pottery?" I said, "I don't know." But I did make money. The shop at the corner of Georgia and Denman Streets took everything I made.

I also used the big gas kiln to fire my sculptures, which were becoming more and more important to me. By my third year studying ceramics, I had pretty much stopped painting; my ideas for paintings became sculptures instead. On assignment, I made a life-size bowler hat adorned with a greenish-brown maple leaf, a purple thistle, a pink shamrock, and a silver rose. (After disappearing from view, this sculpture recently surfaced at the Equinox Gallery.) I also made an Egyptian-paste tap with drops of water in a porcelain saucer, a pile of brownish-red apples, a pyramid of grapefruit, and a work I called *A Washable Cheese Set*, which consisted of a wedge of ceramic cheese on a plate.

Looking at art magazines Glenn brought to class, I saw ways of working in clay that were sympathetic with some of what I was doing, especially drawing on subject matter from overlooked aspects of everyday life. I remember being delighted by Bob Arneson's *Typewriter*, with its slightly grotesque inversion: fingertips for keys. Still, I didn't really identify with the Funk ceramics movement, which was emerging from Northern California in the 1960s. I didn't see my art as confrontational or "vulgar" or satirical. Of course, I also looked at the work of Jasper Johns and Claes Oldenburg, and may have been influenced, unconsciously, by Oldenburg's *Store* project, with its plaster sculptures of shoes, clothes, food, and accessories. Early in my career, when I began exhibiting, my ceramic sculptures were identified with Pop as well as Funk. Still, most of Pop Art wasn't a good fit either, since it was so much about advertising, mass media, and consumerism.

What I made, and still make, is more personal and less slick—more modest, I believe, and more obviously handmade. My art is often called playful or whimsical. I hate the word "whimsy" because it makes it sound as if I just had a lighthearted idea and made it materialize in paint or clay. I think far too much of my work for that to be true. My process *is* intuitive, however. It originates in my surroundings, in my house, my garden, my neighbourhood. More importantly, it jumps out of my imagination. Elements of it are surrealistic—a photo of the Modernist artist Méret Oppenheim's fur-lined teacup totally resonated with me—but without the dogma of the original Surrealists. For me, art is totally a personal working out of images.

HOME
ENVIRONMENT

IN 1966, I BEGAN working on the ceramic sculptures and altered found objects that would be part of my breakthrough installation. It was first titled *Living Room Environment*, but I later changed it to *Home Environment*, which was more accurate and also more succinct. I may not have known it at the time, but I was making a three-dimensional still life, a work with many components, the major themes being furniture, food, clothing, and games.

On the last day of 1967, Doug Chrismas invited me to show in his gallery, a thrill and an honour since the Douglas Gallery was the most progressive exhibition space in Vancouver at the time. I had a couple of months to come up with an idea, and originally I thought of creating an attic setting. Then I realized that a number of the sculptures of household items I'd already made would fit into a living room environment. ("Environment" was what installation art was then called.) I'd altered some found furniture and made other pieces of furniture out of clay—very delicate.

Pink Chair and Fish. Detail from *Home Environment,* 1968. Found objects, enamel paint, flock, varnish, ceramic, 104.1 × 102.0 ×80.0 cm.

The owners of the nearest paint store didn't know (and eventually could not believe) what I was doing with gallon after gallon of pink paint. I was transforming an ugly green 1950s armchair into a hard, glossy sculpture. I had discovered that by repeatedly soaking fabric—either upholstery fabric or clothing—in undercoat and then covering it with enamel paint, I could mimic the appearance of glazed ceramic, which helped marry the found objects with the objects I was sculpting. The handmade ceramic pieces included a checkerboard with alternating pink-flocked and brown-glazed squares and an orange and a woman's shoe on top, another game board with a sandwich on top, a plucked and eviscerated chicken that sat in a birdcage, a frozen TV dinner, a pair of women's shoes encased in resin, a "canvas" side chair with a man's tie draped over it, and folded men's suit jackets mounted in a Plexiglas case.

I screen-printed wallpaper with repeated images of food on plates, including a main course of a chicken drumstick, mashed potatoes, and peas, and a dessert of pie and ice cream. One armchair ended up with flocking all over it. Flocking is the fuzzy stuff you used to see on old-fashioned Christmas cards, and I had found a great source of it in a decorating store located in a back alley downtown. Apart from a bright red sideboard, which I later incorporated into a performance piece, most of the objects in the show were covered with glaze, paint, and/or flocking in grey and light peachy pink. I placed two iridescent grey ceramic fish on the arms of the big pink chair.

The Douglas Gallery was big, but I managed to fill it. The show was titled *Living Room, Environmental Sculpture and Prints*, and the opening reception was spectacular. I wore a peachy-pink dress that I'd made for the occasion. The gallery was jammed with visitors, so many that they ended up spilling out onto the Davie Street sidewalk. Both of the daily papers covered the show, as did the national arts magazine *artscanada*, and I was interviewed on CBC Radio. The writers who turned out—Ann Rosenberg,

Joan Lowndes, Richard Simmons, and Marguerite Pinney—all enthused about it. And although I didn't make any money from the show (at the time, I sold only one item, a ceramic sculpture of a package of ground beef tied with a string, to an American tourist), my installation was a huge professional success. Critics and curators loved it. I was invited to stage a version of it at the Newport Harbor Art Museum in California, and invitations for other shows and commissions quickly followed.

I was launched.

BEFORE I ALTERED the big old armchair, I sat in it and thought, "Hmm, if I put fish here, on the arms, and mount a man's coat above the back, like a canopy, that would create a feeling of a throne, perhaps. It would suggest a king or a father." It wasn't my intention to evoke my own father, but that is what critics saw in the chair and in the installation itself. Darkness, absurdity, grotesquerie, and the ghost of my dead father.

MY

FATHER

WHAT MEMORIES I HOLD of my father are not my own. Most of them have come to me through my mother, who died in 1972. Others came from friends and relatives who had known him as a young man. Because these stories were told such a long time ago, and no one can verify them now, I feel a little uneasy about recording them. But this is what I believe to be true.

Cornelius Falk was born on June 4, 1896, in Russia, in a Mennonite farming community near Orenburg, in the Ural Mountains. My mother told me that she and he were among the first children born there. It was a new settlement, near the border with Kazakhstan, and had hived off the more populous Mennonite farming communities in southern Russia, in what is now Ukraine—or disputed parts of Ukraine. The German-speaking Mennonites had been in Russia since the time of Catherine the Great and had built up the southern lands into large, fruitful farms. As their prosperity increased, so did the size of their

My father, Cornelius Falk, in Russia, c. 1914.
He bequeathed to me his dark hair, strong
facial features, and deep musicality.

families, and by the late 1800s, new land was needed. (It seems that the terms of their original settlement agreement prohibited them from dividing their farms.) Many Mennonites left for Canada or the United States at that time. Others looked east to the Ural Mountains, which separate European Russia from Asian Russia.

At school, my parents were taught in both Russian and German, their mother tongue. In the wealthier Crimea, Mennonites sent their children to finishing schools and colleges, but nobody in the new settlement was prosperous enough for that. I was told that my father wanted to be a doctor, but his mother forbade it because of the expense of a medical education. Instead, he worked as an overseer for a rich landowner.

My father was intensely musical, played the violin and sang, but was most remembered for his great talents as a choral conductor. He travelled widely, conducting both Mennonite and Russian Protestant choirs. As a conductor, he was known to be precise in his movements and yet emotionally powerful in his interpretation. He was a very good businessman and a good talker; people were drawn to him, loved him, and revered him. Or perhaps this is just the myth a family builds around someone who dies too young. Perhaps it's a shining memory my mother consoled herself with through the long years of her widowhood, and one that we, her children, consoled ourselves with too.

My parents married shortly before the First World War. During that war, my father became a medic, which was a non-combatant way of fulfilling his mandatory military service. (The exemption from military service once granted to the pacifist Mennonites had by then been revoked.) He carried the wounded and the dead from the battlefield. When Russia pulled out of the war, my father was anxious to get home to his family. The story goes that he was impatient because the train was not moving quickly enough; he made his way to the locomotive and asked the engineer to speed it up a bit. He may have opened his purse. He probably stoked the fire. He was arrested and served time in jail. When his jail sentence was over, he was exiled for a period to eastern Siberia, but was allowed to bring his wife and young son, my brother Jack, then known as Jacob, with him. My mother remembered a wide, flat land and digging a big hole in the earth. The hole was covered with a roof of branches and sod, and that was their home while they eked out a living farming.

My father loved to travel, and my mother sometimes recounted tales of their journeys to the Black Sea, and through Uzbekistan and Kazakhstan. Back home in Orenburg, my father worked with his brothers and one of my mother's brothers in setting up grain mills, locally and in distant places such as Omsk in Siberia. During the Russian Civil War, following the collapse of the Russian Provisional Government, there were terrible food shortages. The White and the Red Armies battled each other across the country, both of them confiscating food and livestock. In Orenburg, there were frequent raids by one faction or another, and by roaming gangs of hoodlums. Because of their Germanic background, Mennonites were particularly targeted. In some places, despite their pacifist beliefs, they formed defensive militia units to protect their homes, farms, and families.

By the time the conflict was settled, I was told, the country was impoverished. Nothing could be bought, and no seeds were left for the farmers to sow. Starvation was a real threat. My father and my mother's brother were not prepared to let their families starve; they secured goods like flour and sugar the only way they knew how, through contacts in the black market. To evade detection on their expeditions by horseback, they sometimes wore the uniforms of Communist officers. At times they were shot at by sentries, but they managed to evade being wounded or captured. Still, my father's identity became known to the authorities, and one morning in the fall of 1926, a friend burst into the house and shouted, "They're coming to get you! Leave at once!" By then a second son, my brother Gordon, then called Cornelius, had been born. My father wrote a note to my mother's brother saying, "Everything I own is yours." They left with the breakfast dishes still on the table, taking only a few clothes with them in a black wooden suitcase. Not a trunk, a suitcase. They also took a Bible, a songbook, and a shoebox full of worthless czarist money.

Somehow they managed to get to Moscow and secure exit visas, then took a desperately crowded train to the port of Riga on the Baltic Sea. In the past, when I watched the train scenes in *Doctor Zhivago*, I felt like I was reliving passages from my parents' flight across Russia. In Riga, they caught a Canadian Pacific steamship to Canada. The lower decks were crammed with poor emigrants who, like my parents, had left everything behind. Because of the Mennonites' reputation for honesty and hard work, the company extended them credit for their fare—and it was my family's fare that I ended up paying off when I was a teenager. I believe that between 1923 and 1929, some twenty-one thousand Mennonites came to Canada from Russia. In 1929, they were no longer permitted to leave, and many of those remaining were exiled to Siberia or killed.

After my parents arrived in Canada, they settled first in Alexander, Manitoba, a little town near Brandon. Friends remember that my father conducted the singing in the house church they attended. To earn a living, he took work as an itinerant labourer. My mother said that he regretted his former life, seeing it as too far removed from the spiritual. He interpreted his new and difficult existence as a chance to redeem himself. He had been offered a position as a music teacher somewhere in the northern United States, my mother told me, but didn't take it because he thought it might lead him in the wrong direction, spiritually and materially.

In early 1928, after I was born, my family moved to Oxbow, Saskatchewan, where my father made an agreement with a fellow immigrant to work together to buy some land. When they got their acres, not yet paid for, they planted a row of trees on the bald prairie as a windbreak. Some fifty or sixty years later, my brother Jack identified that patch of land by the row of grown trees. In November, when I was ten months old, the partners were contracted to haul some logs. The load tipped as they were crossing a bridge, and the logs fell off the wagon and into the river below. My father and his partner went into the water to retrieve them. The weather and the water were icy. He developed a terrible cold, and it got worse and worse. He wouldn't see a doctor, and when he finally agreed to go to the hospital, it was too late. He died of pneumonia on the way. Usually I say, "He died of stubbornness."

My father's death and my mother's helpless poverty coincided with the onset of the Great Depression. Years of hardship followed. In the Mennonite communities where we found shelter and support, everyone was poor. I didn't feel the deprivation of our fatherless situation until I was about seven, when my mother moved us to Winnipeg from a small settlement in Northern Ontario. In the city, I noticed that the children who had fathers—fathers who went to work—had more toys and better clothes and could take part in more activities. They could ride the streetcar, go to movies, maybe even take summer holidays. Until then, because I didn't consciously remember my father, I didn't consciously miss him either. When I was ten or eleven, I had a dream that he came back with toys for us. I associated fathers with good things. For a long time, good things were largely absent from our lives.

EARLY

PERFORMANCE

PIECES

IN 1968, A MONTH before my first big show opened at the Douglas Gallery, my dealer sent each of his artists a message that read, "Make a piece that is exactly one minute long." The note was from Deborah Hay, someone I knew to be a dancer from New York. Doug Chrismas had enrolled me in a workshop with her. I wasn't a dancer and I didn't know what a "piece" was. However, I did know about interdisciplinary art. Through my friends and colleagues Glenn Lewis and Michael Morris, I'd been involved with Intermedia, a pioneering multimedia organization founded in Vancouver in 1967 and based in a warehouse on Beatty Street. I had sat in on their meetings and taken part in some of their projects, so these alternative concepts were not new to me. As an experimental choreographer, Deborah had worked collaboratively with a number of artists in New York, to great acclaim. I was about to discover my affinity for performance art.

Fooling around while rehearsing a performance work at Intermedia in Vancouver, 1969. My friend and mentor Glenn Lewis is to the left and fellow artist Ed Varney, to the right.

For days before the workshop, I thought about what my one-minute piece might consist of. I looked at a glossy red ceramic apple I'd made, which was resting on some red wool in my living room and was topped by a plastic parrot. An image popped into my head of the apple on a turntable, attached to a length of narrow tape. If the turntable were spinning, my mind told me, the tape would wind around the apple. I searched the second-hand stores on Fourth Avenue and found a neat square portable record player. At the same time, I locked onto the spirit of candy-apple red, which I achieved by applying an undercoat of gold and then spraying a shiny, semi-translucent coat of red car paint over it. I painted the record player red and then put the ceramic apple on top of the turntable. I struggled to fasten the tape to it. The apple would not rotate on the turntable unless I held it there. I wasted hours trying to make my vision happen. I failed—at least for a while.

At the hour of presentation, with Deborah looking on, along with the other artists taking part in the workshop and the dancers and art-community members who had volunteered to be our "bodies," I simply dropped pieces of my pottery—defective pieces that I couldn't sell—onto the floor. Most of the pottery smashed. After everyone had done their pieces, Deborah told us we had all failed to follow her instructions. We had all gone over our allotted minute. Even I, with a watch in my hand, had run long.

Deborah laid out some rules for us. Each piece had to have a clear beginning and a clear ending. It had to be interesting without being a story, although it might contain some story elements. We had ten minutes to improvise another piece, which was to be based on the sound of our voices. I asked all the people present to give me their shoes, and I put them in a pile. I said, "It starts now." I picked up two shoes at random, placed one on the floor and said, "One," and then I counted ten floorboards and put down the next shoe and said, "Two." I went back to the pile and picked up two more shoes, counted nine floorboards, then eight; two more shoes, counted seven floorboards, then six; and proceeded that way until I saw that I was coming to a wall. At the wall, I turned at a right angle and kept counting and placing the shoes until the pile was entirely gone and the shoes made an L-form. Then I stood up straight and said, "This is the end." It was a lovely moment. Deborah thought my piece was marvellous. To me, the performance process felt very natural. It was like music. I felt myself getting into the rhythm of it.

For the two weeks of the workshop, we were given different problems to work on at home, to be performed the next day, along with another new work. There was one assignment that none of us could do. We made Deborah do it instead. It involved standing in one spot and shrugging a lot. Maybe I was too determined to entertain to find shrugging my shoulders an interesting exercise. Few people from the Vancouver workshop continued doing performance art then, although A A Bronson went to Toronto, where he became a member of the General Idea collective and greatly enlivened the art scene there. Glenn Lewis and the Western Front group did a lot of performance through the 1970s, taking their art in many creative directions.

In my performance art, which I worked on (along with my ceramic sculpture) for the next half-dozen years, I liked to use ordinary, everyday activities: eating an egg, reading a book, drinking tea, washing my face, putting on makeup, cutting hair. I also liked to incorporate slightly more exotic elements, such as shining someone's shoes while he was walking backwards and singing an operatic aria; sewing cabbage leaves together; using a ruler to knock ceramic eggs towards real eggs, as if in a game of croquet; and sawing popsicles in half and using them as weapons. Critics have noted that there is a sense of ritual in my work. In fact, there is a sense of ritual in my daily life.

Sometimes a piece develops in a linear way with one event following another; at other times, the choreography is worked out like a fugue, with one event beginning close upon the heels of another and a third event intertwining with the first two. One of my performances, *Red Angel*, is like a rondo, with theme A followed by theme B, followed by theme A again. *Red Angel*, which I first performed in 1972 wearing a wedding dress and a pair of big, white, feathered wings, is the work in which I was able to realize my vision of shiny ceramic apples rotating on shiny red turntables. In this piece, each apple was surmounted by a plastic parrot, also painted red. At a certain point in the performance, I shed the wedding dress, revealing a grey satin gown beneath. The wedding dress spent time sloshing around in an old-fashioned wringer washing machine, operated by my friend Elizabeth Klassen. Again, as in a rondo, the first theme was repeated at the end.

As with my work in other media, the ideas for all my performances came unbidden—but not whole, not perfect. I have to work quite consciously on the germ of an idea to craft it. To some viewers, it seemed that all the effort directed into my performances was made with a view to toppling the usual order of things. Or that the aim was outrageousness. Not so. The actions and props I used belonged together in that mysterious way that all things in every strong work of art belong together, with neither too much nor too little of anything. I was not fighting the battles of the Dada artists; in fact, I wasn't fighting any battles, just creating with new material the things I also made in more traditional media. The new material was people.

Things didn't always go as planned. The audience was often stoned, their minds blooming on another planet. (Sometimes the performers were stoned too, and were deluded into thinking that the drugs improved their work. They didn't.) The first time that my friend Tom Graff and I did a performance together, someone came up from the audience and started taking off his clothes. I had been placing teacups on the floor, and Tom was wrapping a chair with shiny aluminum foil. There was dramatic tension between these two acts, and then this fellow I'd never seen before inserted himself into the middle of the work. He took his shoes off, then his wristwatch, then his jacket. People thought this was part of the performance. It was not. Tom got up and yelled, "Stop it! I don't ruin your work—don't ruin ours!" The guy fled down the aisle, and Tom threw his shoes, coat, and watch after him. Our performance resumed. Later on, I noticed our interloper creeping around, looking for one of his articles. Then he vanished. I never saw him again.

I like to work collaboratively with other artists and friends, but I am not interested in unfettered audience participation. For a while, there were "happenings" at the Vancouver Art Gallery, although I didn't take part in them and I found them boring to watch. On one occasion, at the opening of an Intermedia exhibition at the Vancouver Art Gallery, the Plexiglas and shredded-paper sculpture I was exhibiting was destroyed during a spontaneous happening. Paper was torn from the bales I had incorporated into my sculpture and strewn all over the gallery. I was furious, but there was nothing I could do. By contrast, my performance works were not based on chance; they were carefully designed, composed, and rehearsed.

MY

MOTHER

IT IS, FOR ME, a scary thing to write my mother's story. She has been gone for so long and her life was so entangled with mine, so much a part of my own story for so many years, that trying to get a sense of the whole of it is daunting. I still grieve at all that she suffered.

She was born Agatha Penner on May 8, 1894, in the same place as my father—a numbered but unnamed Russian Mennonite settlement near Orenburg. Her childhood was deeply troubled. Her mother, whom she always fondly remembered, died when she was four or five. Her father remarried, had more children, and was widowed again. He married a third time, a woman not much older than my mother, and had still more children. In all, he fathered more than twenty children, perhaps as many as twenty-three. The one my mother felt truly attached to was her older sister, her own mother's first child. One of our heartless childhood entertainments was to ask Mother to name all her siblings. Gordon and

My mother, Agatha Falk (née Penner), and I in Winnipeg,
1942. During the war our financial situation eased
somewhat, allowing us the luxury of a studio portrait.

I wanted to know exactly how many there were. When she caught on to us, she said she would never again count all her father's children. And she kept her word.

Her father wasn't rich, but he had a large farm and was also the administrator of the settlement. He was well thought of in the community, but not by Mother. She was furious at him for having so many children, particularly because she and her older sister were forced to look after them all. She escaped this unpaid domestic labour by taking a job as a servant in my father's family's household, where there were six grown-up children—and no little ones. And there was music. My father and all his siblings sang and played musical instruments. My mother brought very little with her to Canada, but she did bring a handwritten songbook. The songs were recorded in the way of that time and place: instead of notes, there were numbers on a staff. Much later my mother and I sang a lot of those songs together, in her native German language.

When I was young, my mother and I would often sit at the table after lunch, and I would ask her about her life in Russia. When I asked her once whether she had been in love with my father, she surprised me by saying no. What? "I was in love with his older brother, but he married someone else," she said. Still, I know she was terribly attached to my father and admired him deeply. In Winnipeg, when I was growing up, I had witnessed her crying and telling the other women in our community about her first husband and what a wonderful person he was. So much of her past was painful to her—as was her present—but she seemed happy to tell me stories about my parents' expeditions together. I learned that the extended family would go on bathing holidays to the Caspian Sea. This involved a long journey by horse-drawn carriage, with the beautiful Ural Mountains as a backdrop. In my mind, when she described it, I could see the luminous dust, shot through with golden sunlight. At the seaside, the menfolk would bathe in one spot and the women in another. I liked to imagine them returning in the evening and its ecstatic elements—the moon, the mountains, the singing.

My mother spoke about the friendly nomadic people she and my father met on their travels in Kazakhstan and Uzbekistan. The nomads, she told me, had no cows; instead they milked their horses, even making cheese from the mares' milk. My parents enjoyed the people and the food. But not all their journeys were pleasurable. Exile with my father in eastern Siberia was their first great hardship. And my family's desperate flight out of Russia, with their two sons, was—of course—a nightmare. What was hardest on my mother, physically, was the steamship voyage to Canada. She was terribly seasick the entire time, including the stop in England. For years afterwards, she wanted to return to her loved ones in Orenburg. Only the prospect of another sea voyage stopped her from going.

And then, when my mother was thirty-four, my father died. There's a black-and-white photograph of our bereaved family, taken in Oxbow, Saskatchewan, just before my father's funeral. It was shot outdoors, beside an unadorned plank house, with a view of wide, snow-covered fields beyond. The focus is on an open casket, tipped up so that the body, dressed in a dark suit, is clearly visible. The chief mourners—my mother, my brothers, and I in my mother's arms—stand behind the casket. An unidentified man, possibly my father's partner, stands off to the far right. Photos much like this one came by post from Russia fairly soon after, and again much later. It was no shock to us to see yet more evidence of death, bodies laid out on embroidered white cloths in plain wooden caskets, family members standing nearby.

People did their best for us in Oxbow, but they were all poor immigrants and had difficulty even supporting themselves. A worldwide financial crisis had begun, and a decade of economic depression. There really wasn't any work for many people, and certainly not for my mother. Other families sheltered us for brief periods of time, but my mother was frequently on the move trying to find a place for us to live. She moved us back to Manitoba, first to Winkler and then to Hochfeld, a Mennonite farming community in the far south of the province, near the border with North Dakota. We were taken in by a family at the older end of the village, which had been founded in the nineteenth century. They were very kind people—very, very kind—but we couldn't stay with them forever. Somehow they found us a house at the other end of Hochfeld, where newly settled Russian Mennonites lived.

My mother worked in the fields by day and looked after us the rest of the time. She sorely missed her older sister, who, with the rest of the large family, was still in Russia. For a few years, there were letters and photographs from home, but then Stalin put a sudden end to all correspondence with foreign countries. My mother was not to know the agonies of Christians living in a communist state until after Stalin died.

In Hochfeld, we had a cow and chickens—by what good fortune, I do not know. Still, my mother struggled to support us. I remember running into the house one day when I was about five, yelling, "The chicken laid an egg! The chicken laid an egg!" And my mother saying, "Shush, shush, quiet." There was a man there, a red-haired stranger, and she introduced him to me. This was the man who would become her second husband. He had placed an advertisement in the Mennonite weekly newspaper, my mother had answered it, and now he had travelled from his home in Reesor, in Northern Ontario, to meet her. He was a widower with five children, two boys and three girls. After that visit, he returned to his home. He and my mother must have corresponded some more; a few months later, we took the train to Reesor and they were married. I think my mother was looking for economic security, but it was all too quick. She didn't really know the man she married. She didn't ask whether he drank.

I wasn't aware of his drinking, but I knew he didn't like me. He thought I was spoiled, he spoke to me sarcastically, and he wouldn't let me touch him. His children were allowed to play with him on Saturday mornings when he sat reading the paper, but I was not. Still, I was young and oblivious enough to find pleasure in the two years we spent in Reesor. It is a ghost town now, but then, in the early 1930s, it was a thriving young community founded by Russian Mennonites but also including French Canadians and Finnish immigrants. Its economy was dependent on logging and farming. The trees in that part of Ontario were good only for pulpwood. The soil was thin, and eventually the farming there declined. But that is not something I remember.

The children of my mother's second husband were lovely, very nice and very well behaved. The oldest was Jake, who was sickly and needed my mother's frequent attention at night. Tina was a few years older than I, and Mary was my age. Agnes was younger, a whiner, and I had a few scraps with her. The youngest, Danny, was a dear—no trouble at all. The girls all went to bed at the same time, all four of us sleeping crossways with Danny at the end. Until we were told to be quiet and go to sleep, my stepsisters and I would sit up in what seemed to me an enormous bed and sing all the hymns we knew. There was one hymn I wasn't allowed to sing because it had been their mother's favourite. I knew it but I wasn't allowed to sing it.

Tina, Mary, and I liked to fuss over my mother. We wanted to comb her hair, which was brown and wavy, and when taken out of its tidy bun—the high bun all the married Mennonite women wore—fell well below her shoulders. I loved the look and feel of it, but we were only allowed to comb it when we had a cold or some minor ailment that granted us special status. When my stepfather was away, we also got to sleep with my mother. These events were infrequent.

It was during my mother's second marriage that we children began to see her as sickly. Previously, she had always been well and strong, but in Reesor, she became ill and had to go to a hospital in Southern Ontario. Her illness was never explained to us. Later in her life, she was hospitalized a number of times, equally mysteriously. Occasionally I wondered if her ailment was psychosomatic. When I was in my thirties, I finally asked her what it was. "Women's problems," she said. "You don't need to know." And I didn't know. I still don't.

One day when my stepsisters and I were playing hide-and-seek in the house, I opened the door of the tall built-in closet in our bedroom. To my astonishment, my mother was sitting inside, on the edge of a shelf, crying. This was the first time that I could recall seeing her cry. Of course she would have wept when my father died, but I had no conscious memory of it. She looked shocked that I had found her in such a demeaning state. I shut the door quickly so the others wouldn't see.

My stepfather drank with our neighbour, the schoolteacher. When he came home from a night of drinking, he would treat my mother very roughly. Once, after she had begged our neighbour to throw out all the liquor or hide it, my stepfather choked her. She told me later that she was sure he was going to kill her. He also beat my older brother. I remember the horror of hearing him thrashing Jack out in the yard, and Jack's cries of pain and anger.

My mother must have spoken with friends in the church about my stepfather's drinking. One November day, while he was out, she told us to put on our coats and took us away. She cried when she kissed her stepchildren goodbye, and they cried too. We walked towards a house of friends a couple of miles away, our first place of refuge. Gordon and I didn't know what was happening and were having a good time jumping around, breaking the ice on the puddles, laughing. In a sudden outburst, my mother told us to stop it, told us this wasn't a game. She was extremely sad. Jack knew what was going on, and he was very quiet. That first night away, when I was sleeping on a bed of blankets on the floor, I was awakened by my stepfather's angry voice. He was trying to get my mother to come back, but she refused. The people we were staying with didn't want her to go either. He left. I wet the bed that night, to my great shame and horror.

We stayed at the first house for a few days and then moved to another. Jack and Gordon and I were still going to school, a one-room log cabin where I learned to read but not much more. We walked together with other children in the November darkness. Once we saw a fox and, startled, pulled close to each other. After a couple of weeks, my mother and Gordon and I took the train to Winnipeg, where we had distant relatives, cousins of my father's. They were not well off either, and not too pleased to see us. Still, they did help us for a while. We had no money. Jack had to stay behind in Reesor and do logging work, essentially as an indentured labourer, to pay off what we had borrowed for the train fare.

It took great courage and resolution for my mother to leave her husband. It was unusual for the time and for her community. The Mennonite women sympathized with her, but the men believed it was her duty to remain in the marriage. The separation may have spared her and her family a lot of misery, but it also impoverished her again and coloured her life grey for many years. Shortly after arriving in Winnipeg, Gordon and I played a game, recalling our time in Reesor. Gordon drew a map of where we had lived and where we had gone to school. We were energetic and probably noisy. The three of us were living in one tiny room, and my mother, distressed and angry, laid down a new law: "Never ever talk about that time or anybody who lived there!" We were taken aback. I obeyed her proscription for many years, until we left Winnipeg.

Poor as we were, we children were always well fed and neatly dressed in homemade clothes. We lived in a clean and tidy house, often filled with delicious cooking and baking smells that I will forever associate with my mother. She was a very good cook, and the flavours of my childhood include the cabbage rolls she made in a saucepan on top of the stove. She would brown the rolls and simmer them for hours, turning them over often and adding water so that there was a lot of flavourful gravy at the end. She also made crepes, standing at the stove and serving them to Gordon and me "hot off the grill." We ate them with sugar and cinnamon, or just as they were, without condiments.

Another terrific dinner was homemade *vareniki*, which are similar to perogies. My mother rolled out the soft pasta dough, cut it in circles, and folded the circles into half moons over fillings of cottage cheese and egg, or of fruit, often saskatoon berries that we had picked and she had canned. If we were lucky, there was *schmaunfat*, a delicious sauce of browned butter and cream. Again my mother stood at the stove cooking while we ate the vareniki, hot from the pot to our plates. She was truly selfless in serving us this way. She ate after all the food was cooked, much of it consumed, and she could sit down to what was left.

Mother's cabbage borscht, not one of my favourite dishes, was unusually heavy on hot peppers and fat. Every bit of fat had to be eaten. Meat was expensive, and maybe it was important for poor people to build up their children with fat instead. My mother had a high tolerance for the chili peppers, but if my brother bit into a piece of one, which when cooked resembled a bit of tomato, he would rise up in the air and run yowling around the house. I encountered fewer peppers because I ate as little soup as I dared and chose carefully among the red bits. And there was homemade bread to fill up on instead.

We seldom drank tea, but when we had it on Sunday afternoon, we drank it light coloured with a blob of raspberry jam at the bottom of the cup. This was a makeshift way of serving tea; the traditional Russian way was to drink it from a glass, perhaps with a silver handle and, again, a spoonful of jam. At special times, tea was served with lemon and sugar. Tea and baking-powder biscuits made a satisfying Saturday dinner after a day of much baking to supply the food we would eat on Sunday, and for a couple of somewhat more meagre days after that. Saturday dinners might also consist of Ukrainian sausage (with lots of garlic) and boiled potatoes. Another simple meal was fried potatoes and green tomato sauce. I assume this tasted much like French fries and ketchup. Not exactly healthy, but certainly delicious.

My mother was also a gifted seamstress and resourceful craftsperson, creating new things out of old. She made shoes, the uppers fashioned out of cloth, and the soles, of tightly braided twine. And she once made a rug for her bedside from some old woollen coats, which she took apart and then sewed together again, flat. She stitched an edging of satin on it and appliquéd big flowers—red petals with yellow centres and green leaves. Streaming out from the flowers were long embroidered lines. It is a most beautiful rug, so bright and honest and inventive. I still treasure it.

The government, like the Mennonite elders, believed my mother should return to her husband in Ontario. Because she refused to, we didn't qualify for social relief payments, just a tiny subsidy to cover our food. My mother worked occasionally, and so did my brothers, and I, too, when I was old enough. Still, it was the Depression and employment was scarce.

My mother never learned English, so we children would write notes for her, and sign them too. Our relationship with her seemed to shift: she still managed domestic duties, but we had to negotiate the outside world for her, assuming more and more responsibility for adult things—things that I shrank from. Of course I understood the necessity and I did those jobs, even if I didn't want to.

If we needed anything major, like new shoes or a winter coat, we had to go to an office in the provincial legislature buildings and formally request it. I was small, and the clerks couldn't see me as I stood in front of the tall counter in that government office. I learned that I had to take a seat farther down the room so that I was visible when someone else came in. Then I could present our request, our modest petition for, say, firewood. Firewood was cheap, but still it required money. If we were successful in our petition, a cord of wood could be delivered to us the following week.

As I grew older, and certainly by the end of our time in Winnipeg, I started to wonder about some of the things my mother said. They seemed fantastical. In Vancouver, where I continued to live with her and support her for many years, her placid, friendly temperament began to change. She was angry and argumentative and would disagree with me about everything, always taking a negative view of subjects we discussed and saying nasty things to me. I would turn my face to the window, not wanting her to see my tears. Then I would head for my bedroom, where I could let the tears flow freely. Her behaviour became more and more erratic and unpredictable. She insisted that we move frequently because she had developed a hatred for wherever we presently were living. One of our landlords told me that she was crazy and I should put her in an asylum. He told me that while I was at work, she had beckoned to him from her window. He suggested that her gesture was sexual. I found this hard to believe. She had never been interested in suitors. What could it mean? All I could do was cry.

For almost all of my life with my mother, she forbade me the use of the kitchen. That was her domain. But then she started to be muddled about recipes—not always, but episodically. I began to help in the kitchen.

And Mother would fly into rages; she would say things that couldn't possibly be true. There was an incident about a knife that she claimed she had found under her pillow, and she was sure her cousin had put it there. She slept during the day and walked around the house all night. I didn't know what was happening, and I felt fear, grisly fear. I started sleeping with a chair shoved up against my bedroom door. She was losing her memory and her sanity, erratically and incurably, but I didn't know what was wrong until after she died. I didn't know that she had Alzheimer's disease.

My mother loved going to church, but during those years I began to fear she would stand up at some point in the service and say something awful. She never did. I was afraid to invite friends into our home, fearing another of her angry outbursts, afraid again that she would say or do something dreadful. But when I occasionally did have someone over, she was very pleasant. She made the coffee and I served it. While my friends and I talked, she sat in the dining room reading her paper or preparing letters.

After Stalin died and letters could move again to and from Russia, she had continued corresponding with her older sister. I've looked at my aunt's letters, trying to remember her name. Not one is signed. My mother always addressed her sister as *Meine Herzens geliebte Schwester*—"My Heart's Most Beloved Sister." In 1962, my mother's sister died, and her daughter wrote and sent a photo of her burial rites. A slightly earlier photo that I cherish is of my aunt in old age standing in her garden. She is very thin and somewhat dishevelled but lovely. Behind her is her daughter, Liese, and behind them both is the huge old barn, attached to the house in the same Russian-Mennonite style I remembered from Hochfeld.

Every day when I came home from teaching school, my mother demanded to know why I had taken so long. She didn't understand the time it took to mark papers, make lesson plans, and set up science projects. One summer in the early 1960s, I was away for a week and a half attending a summer art camp organized by Jim MacDonald. My mother hadn't objected before I left, but when I got back, her face was ashen and her eyes were circled in dark blue. She looked frightened, terrified, exhausted. After that, because she was so unhappy at being alone in the house, I would take her to a friend's or have someone come in to be with her.

In 1965, I took two months' holiday in Europe with my friend Elizabeth, and arranged for another friend, Mary, to stay with my mother. Things were not easy between them: my mother's behaviour was too difficult, too demanding, angry, forgetful, and fearful. When I returned from Europe, Mary told me something had to be done. Again, I didn't know what was wrong or how to find help. I was probably in denial that things were as bad as they were, but I was also ignorant about Alzheimer's disease and about what support, if any, might be available. The following spring, however, my mother made her own plans. She decided to move into a Mennonite retirement home in Clearbrook, in the Fraser Valley. The director was a friend, and one of her cousins, Renate, worked there. Mother was happy to go to a place where she would never be alone, and with the added benefit of church services. I was relieved but also deeply sorrowing over her departure. In some ways, her leaving felt like a death.

For a while my mother lived very happily in the Mennonite home. She made a good friend there, another old lady, and every day they would run towards each other and hug. Renate thought it was sweet. Then my mother began doing things that made Renate very cross. She started cutting up her new stockings. This didn't seem too serious to me, since they were Mother's own stockings bought with her own money. The scissors were hers too. But other weird things occurred, things that were never described to me but were deemed unacceptable. Dementia was not tolerated by the other residents, or by the staff. My mother, I was told, had to move. I will never forget holding her arm as we made our way out of the building, through two lines of old women who looked on, not with sympathy but with some kind of horror. Perhaps they were afraid that, one day, they too would be led out of their lovely residence, dependent and demented, never to return.

I found a private home for my mother, where she was cared for by a warm-hearted couple, the Friesens. They looked after her and a severely disabled ten-year-old child who lived in a crib and couldn't speak. My mother took a strange dislike to this child and would slap him when she passed by him on the way to the bathroom. After a while, she refused to use the bathroom and had a chamber pot in her bedroom. When she got angry, the old family photos I'd brought from home would end up in the chamber pot, a loss for all of us. Still, when I came to visit, she was on her best behaviour. We would have tea in the dining room, and I would take her out to a nearby park. We would walk arm in arm. She had little to say but was pleasant enough. After a couple of years, though, the Friesens could no longer look after her. There were more episodes with the chamber pot, most of them unspeakable. I was once again looking for a home for her.

My brother Jack had been visiting Mother regularly too, and he was also in agony about what to do. We both knew that I could not care for her while working full-time. I phoned every possible private nursing home—and they were numerous. For some years I had been part of a church group that sang at these places. The elders were always delighted to see us and hear us, but nowhere could I find a nursing home for my mother. Bitterly, I made arrangements for her to be admitted to Valleyview, which was then the provincial hospital for geriatric psychiatry patients. It was part of the Riverview Hospital psychiatric complex in Coquitlam, and definitely considered a place of last resort. Jack took our mother there, and we both visited her frequently. I would stop at the coffee shop on the grounds, buy some goodies and two cups of coffee, and bring them to my mother. A nurse there knew my mother's old gospel songs. She would sing the words, and

Mother, having forgotten the lyrics, would sing the tune, la-la-la. I, of course, added a third voice on those happy occasions. Music remained deeply pleasurable for Mother, but the days when she would blast out the "Hallelujah Chorus" from Handel's *Messiah* on her record player were long gone.

As time went by, Mother spoke less and less. One day, I asked her if she knew who I was. Ever wily, she said, "You are pretty." While she was still mobile, I would take her out in the car for a drive. There were problems caring for her, especially with bathing. She fought the attendants, fearful that she was going to drown. Then she had surgery to repair a hernia that was troubling her, and after that was bedridden for the rest of her life. When I visited her, I fed her with my own hands but I had stopped singing to her, which I later deeply regretted. She was in a large ward, with beds in two rows along opposite walls. The other women seldom, if ever, had visitors. Someone would call out, "George! George! George!" Others talked to themselves. Apart from these brief outbursts, it was mostly quiet there. They all could have done with a song or two.

Late one night, in 1972, there was a phone call from Valleyview. My mother had suffered a heart attack in her sleep and died. I wept and wept at her funeral. My friends and family could hardly believe my sorrow. Mother, after all, was released from her troubles. How could I explain to them that I wasn't crying because of her death?

I was crying because of her life.

Tom Graff and I in front of a thrift shop in Saskatoon, 1971. Wielding the camera and faintly visible
in reflection is Elizabeth Klassen, who joined us
in researching thrift shops across Canada.

THRIFT
SHOPS

ONE SUMMER, MY FRIENDS Tom Graff and Elizabeth Klassen and I went on a mission to research Canadian thrift shops. It was 1971, and we were all avid thrift-shop patrons. Sometimes we made trips to Victoria to look through the shops there, which were better stocked and less picked over than those in Vancouver. Our plan was to visit a few other Canadian cities—Saskatoon, Montreal, Toronto, and Ottawa—to rate the quality of the merchandise we found in their thrift shops.

Tom and Elizabeth were living with me during this period, and we timed our trip to coincide with Elizabeth's two-week holiday from work at a home for the elderly. We funded the trip ourselves, travelling by train, staying in low-end hotels or student housing wherever possible, and making other accommodations to fit our tiny budget. The project was Tom's and mine, and Elizabeth happily acted as our assistant when we needed her help.

I suppose this undertaking could be seen, now, as an early Conceptual Art project, although I don't think that is how we understood it then. It was a bit of a lark, but it was also a structured undertaking with a fixed form and time frame. We were to record our finds and the shops with a camera, the black-and-white photographs to be mounted in an album. At each place we visited, Tom and I had to pick out the best and worst thing in the shop and photograph them. There was also a category for the "most engaging" item. We also photographed the exterior of the shop, with Tom and me front and centre.

Our first stop was Saskatoon, home of the very best thrift shops—with the possible exception of Montreal. We valued shops with a large variety of goods, especially high-quality goods, well made, delightful to us—and priced cheaply. Our camera, an old Leica, was troublesome and, of course, provoked a few fights when we couldn't get it to work. I remember a brisk discussion about loading the camera, with quite a few hard words exchanged at a Saskatoon bus stop. We stayed overnight with Charmian Johnson, and to round out our day of cultural endeavour, Tom sang an opera aria in a huge wheat field, to the delight of the audience, Charmian's artist friends.

In Montreal, every hotel room was booked for conventions. Tom could have stayed at the YMCA but gallantly refused to desert us. We decided to spend the night in a churchyard we had seen while looking around downtown. Before accepting this hard fate, we decided to use our night's hotel money on a good dinner. The dining room at the Queen Elizabeth Hotel exceeded our expectations. Filet mignon? Is it possible? It was an extremely sumptuous meal for budget travellers. Then came preparations for the night. We went to the hotel washrooms, where we jostled the other after-dinner guests for space, soap, and hot water. We washed not only our hands but also our faces. We combed our hair and dabbed on moisturizer. In the toilet stalls, we added layers of clothing, and then headed for the churchyard.

We made beds for ourselves out of our light summer coats and lay down under some bushes, at a little distance from one another. Elizabeth slept well, Tom slept some, and I slept not at all. Every so often I could hear the boom of an underground explosion: Montreal was building a new subway line in anticipation of the Olympic Games that the city would host in the summer of 1976. Other unfamiliar city noises also kept me awake, and then, a little before first light, there was a crunching sound on the gravel path through the churchyard. Tom and I both started up, listening. A man passed near us, paused, returned, stood for a while, and then left. My mind was full of stories of axe murderers who, sensing potential victims, would soon return with vile weapons. Tom was scared too. We woke Elizabeth, scrambled into our coats, and took off for the train station, where we lay on the wooden benches in the waiting room until we were hauled into a sitting position by unfriendly security guards. You were allowed to "wait" in the waiting room, but you certainly could not sleep there. Having spent the entire night awake, I felt like a wilted lily, unable to sit up straight and wait for the day to begin.

We finally scooted out of the safety of the train station and proceeded to spend the day walking from one end of the city to the other. The Salvation Army thrift shop we found downtown outshone our most extravagant dreams. There, we encountered a large and various mass of gorgeous and awful discards. After much happy searching and appraising and a little photographing, I found a clutch of old, thin silver bangles, of a type that had been common when I was young. I bought these as a cheap token of our travels. We then walked up Sherbrooke Street, where many art galleries were located. In and out and up and down, our aching limbs carried our exhausted bodies. We bypassed the major public galleries, seeing that we were on that day's strict budget and couldn't afford the admission fees. Then, having seen all we could, we dragged ourselves back to the station and caught a train to Toronto.

In Toronto, our thrift shop investigations continued, although perhaps with less fervour than at the beginning of our journey. Method was important and we adhered to it: careful looking, careful choosing, careful photographing. There was surprisingly little disagreement about our choices.

The last leg of our journey took us across the Prairies in daylight. We enjoyed the observation car at the end of the train to the fullest. I gazed raptly as we travelled through the foothills, heading towards the Rockies. Right there, an idea seized my mind: clouds moving up and down on strings. The following winter, this kernel of creative matter would become a performance piece—the most tangible thing to come out of our trip.

After we arrived home in Vancouver, we looked through our contact prints and quickly lost interest in the documentary end of our project. It seemed far too dull. Instead of developing the photos and putting them in albums, I turned to making a few short 8 mm films, completely unrelated to our thrift-shop trip. One of the films recorded a performance I called *Landscape Painting*. On a patch of undeveloped land where the Arbutus Shopping Centre is now, I measured out a rectangle with string. I set up my small camera and filmed myself spraying the foliage in the measured rectangle a bright shiny red. Working on my own, without any help, this project took a few days to accomplish. In a later incarnation of the work, I repeated the performance on video, shot with the help of others. The memory of it still gives me a lot of pleasure.

Meanwhile, Elizabeth went back to work at the Louis Brier Home, and Tom investigated the feasibility of getting a government grant to fund the creation of performance works and travel them across the country.

We still look at every thrift shop we come across with avid interest, feeling some items, trying on others, sometimes just guessing at sizes. Our wardrobes are probably half-full of second-hand clothes, old treasures worn with pride. And I still have the thin little silver bangles I bought in Montreal. For years I wore them every day, never taking them off. Part of my delight in them was that I remembered seeing and wanting bangles of this type when I was a child—and not being able to afford them. As an adult, I could afford to buy them second hand. The bangles reminded me of what my youthful joy and status might have been. They were nostalgia all tangled up—or bangled up—with deferred gratification.

My brother Jack, in army uniform, and I during
the war. For many years, we had seen little of
him and it was important to have a photograph
as a memento.

MY
BROTHER
JACK

JACK WAS BORN in Russia on November 5, 1919. Although only eight years older than I, he was a solid and dependable force in our family, often assuming a parental role, although at times that role was in conflict with his youth and inexperience. After my father died, when my mother was too poor to support us all, Jack was sometimes farmed out—literally—to friends. He worked for his room and board, and had to grow up very quickly. Despite what must have been a difficult time for him, he was usually kind and patient with me.

When we were living in Hochfeld, Jack organized our games and taught Gordon and me songs and poems he had learned in school. He also directed us in performances of his devising. I was made to stand on a chair, reciting or singing, and had to close my eyes while he "changed the scenery," rearranging what scant furniture we had. He might push a wooden chair across the room, move the calendar from one wall to another, or rehang a paper streamer. When I was good and tired of standing there with my eyes closed, Jack allowed me to come to life and be a star. He was a demanding director. If even one word was wrong, the poem or song had to be repeated over and over until it was delivered correctly. This was a time when there was little praise for children in school. Good work was expected of you, especially if you were bright. When Jack assumed the role of teacher, he passed his own experiences on to Gordon and me.

If my mother was away from home, we three children amused ourselves in simple ways, there being few toys to play with. My brothers used dried fruit in imaginative ways. In the summer, our family would pick locally grown fruit, such as plums, and my mother would dry them and then store them in a cloth bag. When she was out, we got the pieces of dried fruit out of the bag and devised games with them, counting them out, putting them in piles, using them as currency in our invented exchanges, or as prizes in our competitions. Of course we also ate some of the fruit and, in high spirits, scattered pieces around the house. Just before our mother came home, we would scramble to pick them all up and stuff them back into the bag. Mother must have noticed there was less fruit than before, and what was there must have been grimier too, but we were never spanked for our hijinks.

When we were living in Reesor, even though I was going to school and Jack was sometimes there too, we still played school in the evenings, under his direction. We younger kids were made to print out pages of numbers. They tended to run in wobbly lines from top to bottom and off the page. Later on, Jack set us the task of reading about the little red hen and other stories. For a couple of years at Christmas, in our stepfather's family, there were some toys and treats for us, including fruit and nuts. There was no more playing with our food.

In Reesor, Jack's education was often interrupted so that he could earn money for the family. He had to work alongside the men during the logging season, and in the spring and fall, he assisted with the seeding and harvesting. When our mother left her second husband because of his drinking and abusive behaviour, she must have confided in him and depended on him to help her leave. She borrowed money for our train fare from Reesor to Winnipeg, and Jack stayed behind to work to repay this debt. He rarely spoke of that time, but later he did tell me that someone had stolen the guitar he had recently bought, also with borrowed funds. That must have been a bitter debt to repay.

When Jack finally arrived in Winnipeg, he lived with us briefly in the tiny half-duplex we shared with a young couple, and then all of us separated to work at different farms through the summer. When we came together again, at the end of the summer, we had one large room and an anteroom—a mudroom, really—in a rented house that we shared.

On the whole, Jack appeared good-natured about our difficult situation, but he must have suffered a good deal in silence. Occasionally, his even temper was sorely challenged. One day, he was sitting in heavy thought. He looked unhappy. I tried to amuse him by trotting my doll up his arm. He snarled at me but I carried on, attempting to take the sad look off his face. He seized my doll and tore the leg off. I was shocked. How could Jack, dear Jack, have done such a thing to what was then my only doll? For the rest of my childhood, she had to suffer a condition of debility, her repaired leg dangling helplessly.

Late that fall, when I was eight, Jack was dispatched to take me downtown to get a new pair of shoes paid for by the welfare ministry. Instead of riding the streetcar home, Jack decided to use the fare to treat us to a movie at the Roxy Theatre. Afterwards, we walked home in the bitter cold. I wailed that I couldn't go on, and Jack carried me for part of the way, with difficulty. I caught an almighty cold that night, which developed into whooping cough over Christmas. My mother blamed Jack and yelled at him and berated him incessantly. Even after the whooping cough was gone, I remained ill and weak and nobody knew why. I stopped eating. My mother truly thought that I was going to die, and she directed all her fear in the form of anger at Jack. One day he brought home a box of soda crackers for me. They were not something my family was acquainted with, and he must have been advised by friends about what sick people need. Despite this kindness, I could not eat the hard, dry, salty things.

Around this time too, Jack and Gordon undertook the making of a skating rink, ostensibly for my amusement as I convalesced. They hauled water in pails from the community pump and poured it in an L-shape along the frozen ground at the back and side of the house. In making the rink, they must have hauled hundreds and hundreds of buckets of water, which would not have pleased our landlord but certainly pleased their friends. Through a window I could see the heads of my brothers and these boys whizzing by as they skated on the rink every night, and I could hear their shouts of joy and delight. Some of the boys were also invited in to see me, the sick child. I remember one of them looked at me sadly and kept saying, "Too bad." His cousin, who was with him, concurred.

Jack took over my schooling while I was recovering at home. He picked up assignments from my teacher and improvised from there, trying to teach me fractions and, at one point, demanding that I write an essay. "About what?" I asked. "Oh, something about going for a walk," he said. I found little to report. He kept nagging me to make my essay longer. When I returned to school my teacher told me, "We don't write essays in grade two."

For a while, Jack also worked part-time at a local grocery store. This was a period when he was the sole breadwinner in the family and it seemed he could not earn enough for our rent. Then he lost even this meagre job, and I remember a time when we had no food except rice. The social services people were insisting again that we all go back to Ontario. Jack and my mother agreed that they would rather starve. Jack decided to look for work in British Columbia, the prospects in Winnipeg being so dismal. He borrowed a bike and, I believe, sold it, then left in the night, hopping a freight train for Vancouver. He was about seventeen at the time.

For years, Gordon or I walked the mile and a half to the post office to see if Jack had written. There were occasional warm-hearted notes from him addressing me as Gathie, a new appellation. In school I was known as Agatha, and at home I was called by the German diminutive Agatchen. My birth certificate records me as Agata. Gathie stuck. Jack also changed his last name to Nelson, explaining to us that he might get into trouble and didn't want to besmirch the family name. (There was no mention of the besmirching that had already happened when he illicitly sold the bike he had borrowed, or when he and Gordon sold the violin that belonged to my mother's closest friend, Mrs. Friesen.) One of the photos he sent showed him wearing a loose white scarf and dark clothes. His thin face was caught in an awkward moment, talking, so that it looked oddly awry. There was mention of logging work in Northern British Columbia, and also work as a ranch hand, possibly in the Cariboo. Later, he moved to Vancouver and met, wooed, and married Vera Green, from Burnaby. When the war broke out, he enlisted in the army and there was another photo, of beautiful Vera and handsome Jack in his uniform.

In the armed forces, Jack was trained to operate diesel loco-motives. He was also assigned to drive officers about in England and, later, in France. At one point, he was also assigned to drive captured German officers because he knew a bit of German. He reported that his *Plautdietsch*, the East Low German dialect spoken by Mennonite settlers, was sneered at by the snooty officers. They were prisoners of war, but they were treated better than ordinary soldiers.

After demobilization, Jack stopped in Winnipeg on his way back to Vancouver. Gordon had returned earlier, from his posting in Atlantic Canada, and it was a time for rejoicing with family. To Jack's disgust, I was writing my grade ten exams the week he was home. During the day I worked in a packing house, and I wrote the exams for my high school correspondence courses at night, under the supervision of a teacher. Still, we managed to celebrate on the weekend with a couple of bottles of champagne and a drive in the country. Two things became clear to me: driving in the country is tedious and liquor is horrible.

Years later in Vancouver, where Jack and Vera had been living, and where the rest of us all settled in the late 1940s, there were family dinners and picnics. Jack was very good-hearted and built a few walls and laid a basement floor in the first house I bought. He also taught me how to drive when I was living in Surrey. Initially I was walking miles to work each day, but he came out to Surrey daily to speed up my driver's training. Both of us were surprised when, after only a week of lessons, I passed my driving test. I think the examiner must have turned a blind eye to my mistakes. I'm sure he hoped never to see me again.

Jack was a bus driver for a while, and then he gave that up and went into business with a fellow in Pemberton. When that venture went sour, he moved with Vera and their children, Rick and Bonnie, to Sechelt, on the Sunshine Coast, where he found his calling as a builder. Jack had a superlative professional reputation. He closely inspected every aspect of a building's construction, and if one of his employees had done work that didn't meet Jack's high standards, he made sure it was redone. Jack was known for that attention to detail and dedication to quality.

Although I made occasional visits to Sechelt, there were long passages of time when Jack and I were busy with our demanding careers and saw little of each other. And despite our shared experience of a difficult childhood, our opinions on politics, music, art, and other subjects were poles apart. Jack might not have liked my art, but he never put it down. When he and Vera sometimes visited my studio, she would say heartily, "You've sure been working hard!" I took it as a compliment. Jack and Vera were avid travellers, and when he retired, they spent half the year on road trips around the continent or settled for the winter months in Arizona. Later, when his poor health kept him closer to home (and the Canadian health care system), they continued to travel around British Columbia.

Jack stepped up and generously looked after our mother and our brother in their last years. And yes, although he and I disagreed about many things, we liked each other a lot and had many lively conversations. When Mother was a patient at Valleyview in Coquitlam, we would sometimes drive out there together to visit her. Jack would become so absorbed in what I was saying that he would miss the turnoff. Much later, we had some good visits, sitting under the vine-covered arbour at the back of my house.

After his death in 2006, Jack was honoured by the Sechelt community. A new wing of the seniors' hospital, whose construction he had supervised, was named after him: the Jack Nelson Annex. My tribute was much more fleeting. I placed three stems of peach-coloured geraniums on his coffin at his graveside.

Performing *Some Are Egger Than I* at the New Era
Social Club in Vancouver, 1969. This was the first solo
performance work I developed, and the same work that
provoked laughter and puzzlement in Charlottetown
during our cross-Canada performance tour.

SOME
ARE EGGER
THAN I

THE ARTIST I WORKED most closely with in performance was my friend and fellow thrift-shop explorer Tom Graff. Tom is a classically trained singer with a beautiful bass-baritone voice and an artist of exceptional talent. He usually sang in his performances, which tended to be long, baroque, and complicated, involving many media. What he did, I believe, was bash around conventional forms of entertainment until they emerged in a new and different shape. I didn't want to sing solo in my own performances; despite my years of singing lessons, I didn't have the courage. Tom always insisted on great courage. When I incorporated music, it was of the simplest kind that everybody knew, like "Row, Row, Row Your Boat," sung in rounds by a group of us, taped, and played offstage. I also began to make sculptures specifically as props, and to find ways of constructing my performances visually, like paintings.

In 1972, Tom won a grant for us to create new performance work and show it not only in Vancouver but in art galleries across the country. Tom gathered together the people who would do the legwork for the troupe and also perform with us. They were paid for their efforts, although not very much. (I was not paid at all.) I refined older performances and developed new ones.

Working with us in preparation for the tour were our friends and colleagues Anna Gilbert, Salmon Harris, Alicia Hendrie, Pat Knox, Janet Malmberg, and Elizabeth Klassen. For a few months, people came to my house to paint clay oranges, plastic parrots, and tables with removable legs. I used a jigsaw to cut twenty-four clouds out of thin plywood, and I painted them on both sides. I also devised a method of hanging them so that they could be moved up and down individually with fishing line. They hovered above us in *Low Clouds*, an earlier work I revised for the tour. In this performance, four others sat at office desks reading and I sat in the middle of the group at an old-fashioned treadle sewing machine, stitching cabbage leaves together. For *Red Angel*, we made wings covered in chicken feathers. Before we glued them to the foam forms, Elizabeth washed the chicken feathers inside a pillowcase. Unfortunately, the pillowcase came open during the wash. Feathers clung to all our laundry for a good long time afterwards.

I worked avidly on my performances, as did Tom. Early on, we had created works together, but at this point he made his work and I made mine. We each took roles in the other's pieces, but we tried to keep our performance art separate and distinct. Before our tour, there were endless rehearsals at my house: three of us had to learn to march; Salmon had to learn to push a hundred plastic cocktail glasses across the floor with his prone body; Anna, also prone, practised pushing a hundred ceramic oranges across the floor from the opposite direction. Both had to manoeuvre around each other as they herded their flocks of objects while lying flat on the floor, without looking at each other or speaking or touching. I saw this manoeuvre as two trains shunting back and forth, trying to pass each other. Others saw it as the difficulties of communicating between the sexes.

All was not sunshine and light during our preparations. I got very tired of having so many people in the house all day. We started with coffee at my dining room table, worked for a few hours, and then stopped again for lunch. Some people brought their own lunches; others did not. They seemed to expect to be provisioned. Around three o'clock, there was another break for tea. Lots of food prepared and served, lots of dirty dishes, lots of silent grimacing on my part. I got sick and tired, developed stress headaches and an upset stomach. My good friend, the curator Glenn Allison, came by with a Valentine's Day cake for all of us. That made me well again.

Another friend, Max Dean, who went on to become an acclaimed artist himself, built two crates that were excellent for travelling: you could open one up on arrival at an airport, pop out a dolly, and forge ahead to the next connection. All our performance gear fit into those two boxes. A big tape machine travelled separately in its original box.

Our first stop was Charlottetown, where I performed *Some Are Egger Than I*, a work that entailed my eating eggs while seated on a black-and-red pillow. There were cooked eggs in a white bowl on a red table, and raw eggs and gold ceramic eggs scattered on a large piece of white paper on the floor in front of me. I chose an egg from the white bowl, ate it from a gold-rimmed egg cup, got up, picked up a long ruler, surveyed the scene on the floor, chose a ceramic egg and batted it with the ruler towards a real egg, smashing it. Eating and hitting were repeated until all the real eggs were "dead"—consumed by me or lying broken in a puddle of yolks and whites. Simultaneously, a film of a figure in a long dress was projected on a screen behind me. The woman in the film wore workers' goggles and was slowly pelted with raw eggs. In retrospect, I see the piece as being a kind of war game. I had a feeling when I performed it that I was like a general, eating my breakfast peacefully and complacently and then going out and bashing somebody to death with my ruler.

During that particular performance in Charlottetown, an unfortunate gap developed between my white top and my white shorts. Every time I bent over to bat an egg with the ruler, my shorts slid down and the top of my red underpants was revealed. This accidental display provoked much hilarity in the audience— and especially great guffaws from the artist Roy Kiyooka. At the time, I wasn't aware of what was happening. I didn't know the audience was laughing *at* me, not *with* me. Otherwise, I think people were simply puzzled by our efforts. They didn't know what to make of them.

Our next stop was Toronto. The Art Gallery of Ontario was under construction, and so we were taken in by the Isaacs Gallery. Since we couldn't lug everything with us, we bought new dishpans, eggs, cake-making ingredients, etcetera for every performance. We had brought an electric cooking element with us but were depending on gallery owner Av Isaacs to lend us a small pot to cook the eggs in. Each day, for almost a week, he forgot to bring one to the gallery. Finally, harrowed by our demands, he handed over the pot at the last moment. We, harrowed by his delinquency, were much relieved.

In Ontario, even curators and directors of public galleries had trouble understanding what I was doing and why. (Only years later, when my major performance works were recorded on video, did they begin to appreciate what I had brought to the art form.) My performance art was intended to call forth emotions. Some of my work was gruesome; some was a bit thrilling. Some, undoubtedly, was boring to others; some, apparently, was maddening.

We delivered two performances in Toronto, and Av thought we were very professional. The audience sat on chairs in a half circle around us, rather than on cushions on the floor as our audiences in Vancouver did. Av's friends found our efforts entertaining and new. People from another art enclave said we were reworking the Dadaists and therefore were fakes and irrelevant. (Actually, our art history at that time was very weak—we didn't know much about the Dadaists and certainly weren't modelling ourselves on them.) However, after our second show, which took place on a Saturday afternoon, there was a great discussion with the audience, who expressed some anger over our supposed irrelevance. Happily, no blows were exchanged.

Our performances in London, Ontario, were planned primarily because two of Canada's leading artists, Jack Chambers and Greg Curnoe, lived there. The show was booked into an awkward facility—just big enough, but without any comforts or amenities. Tom had spent a lot of time practising a Mozart sonata on his clarinet. I can't fully remember his performance, except that at some point I read the list of ingredients off a chocolate bar wrapper while other things happened around me.

Later, Greg threw a party for us in his marvellous studio, which was in an old storefront. He greeted us warmly but didn't seem to know what to do with us. He phoned Jack and tried to entice him to join us, but Jack was not to be lured away from his comfortable home. We looked at Greg's art, his beautiful paintings of bicycles and bicycle wheels, but conversation lagged, which it often does when artists who don't know each other are thrown together. It didn't seem enough to say, "I love your work." Drinks were offered, which further withered the conversation. Not one of the three of us—Tom, Elizabeth, or I—drank hard liquor. Nor did we smoke. Dead dogs were we. Instead of the full-blown party that Greg had planned, there were early departures and quiet goodbyes. Ironically, Tom would later become close friends with Jack and his wife.

After London, we flew to Calgary. Our work in that city was sponsored by the University of Calgary, and we were billeted there too. My memory is that we were warmly welcomed by the faculty, beginning with a party made lively by instructors who had no idea what they were about to see. Our theatre was the university gym. We did our stuff before a good young audience who seemed very excited by our work.

In the meantime, things had become very strained between Tom and me. Our roles in these foreign places were reversed from those at home. In Vancouver, everyone thought I was the initiator of our separate performance works, a situation that understandably irked Tom. In Alberta, because Tom had organized the tour, it was taken for granted that the work was all his. The local press interviewed him and ignored me. Now *I* was miffed and I blamed Tom for allowing it to happen. There were sniffy times during which Tom took his meals with Janet, and Elizabeth, Salmon, and I ate separately. It sounds childish now, but I guess my ego was bruised.

Our last stop on the tour was in Edmonton, which we reached by bus from Calgary. There were still warlike relations between Tom and me, but we didn't let them interfere with the performances, which took place at the University of Alberta. Westerners seemed to get what we were doing, and again our work was well received.

I don't recall what became of Max Dean's boxes when we got home to Vancouver, but I do remember the gift that Glenn Allison left us. He had been in charge of the house while we were away, and made a gorgeous necklace for me, which he draped over my ceramic sculpture, *196 Apples*. A grand ending to our tour.

MUCH LATER, TOM once more obtained a government grant, this time to record our performances on video. After we restaged them on tape, they were shown at my first big retrospective exhibition, at the Vancouver Art Gallery in 1985, and again in 2000 at my second big retrospective (also at Vancouver Art Gallery). That second show travelled extensively, and I remember that when it was in Ottawa, at the National Gallery of Canada, I looked at the taped performances again—and was flooded with relief. Even now I sigh with relief whenever I think about those tapes. No more need to lug around heavy boxes filled with numberless props, no more looking in vain for a round dishpan in an unfamiliar city, no more teaching a new crew to crow.

My brother Gordon in St. John's, 1944. His
jaunty pose hints at his rapscallion nature.

MY

BROTHER

GORDON

MY BROTHER GORDON led a checkered life. In adulthood, for a
period of about twelve years, he was a model of virtue. He married Edith Smith, a beautiful young woman whom he met in
St. John's, Newfoundland, where he was stationed during the Second World War. They had three children, Bob, Carol, and Susan,
who all adored him. He was an excellent father, very kind to his
children but also able to maintain authority. His oldest child, Bob,
recounted fishing trips with Gordon, and making things together
on Saturdays in the basement shop. I still have and cherish a little wooden stool Bob made with his father and gave to my mother.
The girls were taken camping and on picnics. All of them enjoyed
a loving, stable, cheerful home life. This seems to have been Gordon's golden phase, from a family point of view.

I had known a very different brother and held my breath.

Gordon, who was born in Russia on May 17, 1925, was two-
and-a-half years older than I. We played together frequently and

fought incessantly. I'm sure my mother loved him more than any of us, maybe because, when he was young, he told her everything that happened to him. I did not. I was very quiet at home. I read, I spent a lot of time inside my head, and I kept my lips sealed. In Winnipeg, in the summer, we slept with the doors between our rooms open. My mother and I were in the bigger room, and Gordon, in the smaller one. Gordon and Mother would talk and talk and talk after going to bed. He would tell her a cannily edited version of his life, although he always had adventures to recount. Being a boy, he was allowed to be gone the whole day on holidays and weekends, as long as he came home for dinner. I envied his freedom and didn't see why my being a girl should prevent me from having the same liberty. My mother disagreed with me.

Gordon was named after my father, Cornelius, and was given the nickname Corny as a kid. Because of what it meant in English, he hated it. My mother would say, "Your dad always loved it when the Russians called him Corny because it was a term of endearment." But that didn't mean a thing to him. When he joined the army, he changed his name to Gordon, and Gordon he remained.

Despite his seeming accord with my mother and the delight she clearly derived from him, Gordon had never really accepted the rules everyone else adhered to. When I was in grade two and he was in grade five, we were supposed to walk to school together. As likely as not, he would do his best to make us late. This caused me a lot of anxiety because the first time I was late for school, I was strapped by my teacher. It was a heavy strap and I suffered a good bit, and not just physically. On days when it looked like we were going to be late, I bowed to the less painful option, which was to play hooky with Gordon.

We often spent our delinquent days in the woods, walking through the low bush and eating chokecherries, with me complaining of fatigue and demanding to be carried. Gordon would build a small fire, or if it was raining and the fire sputtered out, we would make for a farmer's warm, dry barn. We had to hide from anyone who would report us to the truant officer. To me—long before my own rebellious and hooky-playing phase—this subterfuge was scary. To Gordon, it was exciting. If we were found out, there would be a great to-do at home. Gordon rightfully bore the blame for our deviant behaviour.

I remember a day of skipped school soon after we moved to North Kildonan, which was about four miles from central Winnipeg. Gordon talked me into spending the day with him downtown, although I wonder now how we got there. It was unlikely we had the five-cent streetcar fare there and back. Certainly, we had no money when we headed home. I remember the long walk back and begging Gordon to carry me part of the way, and somehow he did. During that great adventure, Gordon introduced me to the escalators in Eaton's department store. They were cruder then than they are now, and I felt very uncertain while standing on the moving boards. My brother, of course, was not bothered at all. We then roamed the downtown streets, had little if anything to eat, and returned home late to a furious mother and older brother. There was a lot of yelling, and Jack, who was five-and-a-half years Gordon's senior, punished him with a severe beating. Later, Gordon used to declare that when he was bigger, he would beat the tar out of Jack. He never did.

After that, my trips downtown with Gordon took place on Saturdays. We would start at Eaton's, go up Portage Avenue to the Hudson's Bay store, and then check out the civic museum, looking at the stuffed animals in the basement and trying to make out the pictures in the darkened art gallery on the top floor. Down the street from the museum were the legislative buildings. We would dash in there, running up and down the marble halls, hooting and hollering and hiding behind the pillars. Sometimes

Gordon would sneak into the legislative chamber and sit in the speaker's chair.

Happily, when I was in grade three, we lived close enough to school that Gordon no longer had to accompany me there. That was also when he pretty much stopped going to school. Usually, Mennonite children were well behaved and attended school as long as they could, leaving it only to work to help support their families. At this point, Jack had moved away and our mother seemed incapable of keeping Gordon in line. He had stopped going to church too. Occasionally, he would honour his teachers by making an appearance in school. He was smart and could always solve the math problems set for him. He could read well and astutely too. Perhaps that's why the authorities did not come down hard on him. Or perhaps it was that the truant officer was never able to find him.

Gordon wasn't particularly popular with his classmates, at least not with the boys. He had a tendency to brag, and he often got into fights in the cinder-covered schoolyard. It occurs to me now he may have enjoyed these encounters, but at the time my heart bled for him. For whatever reason, he refused to fit in. And he was a thief. He and Jack borrowed and then sold the treasured violin that belonged to my mother's closest friend, Mrs. Friesen. Her house was my second home, the place I would stay if my mother was ill or in hospital. The stolen violin caused both her and my mother a lot of grief. My brothers were forbidden to ever enter Mrs. Friesen's home again. I think her family was eventually able to recover the violin. Or perhaps that is just a wish, repeated so often that it seems real.

Jack and Gordon would sometimes take the money left in milk bottles on back porches—money left for the milkman. And then there was the matter of the bicycle. How did Gordon get hold of that? It worried me initially, but later, when Gordon taught me to ride on the bike, I stopped inquiring about it. He also regularly brought home piles of newspapers and magazines—back issues of everything from news magazines to movie magazines to *Esquire*—that he probably found near garbage cans. Only recently has it occurred to me that this reading material was not for himself, his tastes running to snakes and other horrors of the Amazon. He chose these publications to feed my insatiable appetite for reading.

It's possible that Gordon took one of the few books I possessed as a child. It was one of the Uncle Remus books, which had been a gift from members of our church when I was deathly ill with whooping cough. The stories were about Brer Rabbit and his kin, and I didn't really enjoy them. They were written in a dialect I didn't understand. Nor did I understand the worries of these Southern creatures, or what the farmer and the fox meant to them. The book, however, was illustrated in colour and had come to me brand new, which was a valued quality. When it disappeared, I suspected Gordon had taken it to give to one of the girls he wanted to impress. Girls seemed much on his mind. He was a handsome boy, and a handsome man, and he was probably on the minds of some girls too.

Some years later, when Gordon was gone a good deal, working for a produce merchant and driving into the countryside to pick up chickens and vegetables for resale in the city, I made a discovery. This was during a period when I was conducting experiments in electricity in our house. Having shocked myself while fooling around with the only light in the room, which hung from the ceiling at the end of an electrical cord, I learned to shut off the breakers in the kitchen. For some reason, we could either have light or play the radio, but not both at the same time. I found a way of solving that problem too, so that I wasn't in the dark when I listened to *The Lone Ranger*. Another problem with the radio had me turning it around, peering into its depths, removing a tube, and finding a new one to insert in its place. That fixed the radio, but what interested me most in this exercise was discovering the notebook hidden inside its cabinet. It was filled with the names of girls, places, and activities that I'm sure Gordon never related to our mother.

I was astonished at my find. It was like discovering an important clue to a mystery, although I wasn't old enough to divine the whole of its meaning. After reading everything, I carefully put the book back in its hiding place. Later, I would look at it occasionally, but it had lost some of its initial savour. Later still, when Jack was home on leave from the army before shipping out to England, I spent an uneasy evening with him. He had been living on the West Coast for many years, and we were not well acquainted with one another. We sat at the kitchen table, self-conscious, tongue-tied, sipping soft drinks. There was a huge lump in my throat, and I was having difficulty swallowing. It seemed to me that I was audibly gulping. Embarrassed, I thought of Gordon's little notebook and imagined it would entertain Jack. I took it out of the radio cabinet and showed it to him. He looked at it, shook his head a few times, and put it back in its place. He didn't talk about it. His silence was chastening. I felt ashamed for betraying Gordon.

From the start, Gordon had a keen engineering mind. He would draw designs of airplanes and make models of them, original models, quite different from the model airplanes all the other boys made from kits. He built igloos in the backyard and constructed a boys' clubhouse in the woods. He also drew bridges in ways that he knew would keep them from falling down. Fifteen years later, without the benefit of a high school or university education, Gordon was designing salmon runs. His plans were very detailed and provided for any contingency. He was working for the forestry department at the University of British Columbia at the time, attending night classes, and, having accomplished a level of knowledge equal to that of the department's graduate students, he applied for a promotion. He wanted to see his salmon runs built and implemented. When he was denied the promotion because he lacked a university degree, he went berserk. He quit his job. He left his family. He broke a lot of hearts and went back to living by his wits.

The salmon runs were later implemented, more or less as Gordon had designed them, but he wasn't here to enjoy—or resent—their success. He had left Vancouver to travel widely through Europe and Africa. He had borrowed money that he could not repay. He had left his family destitute and dependent on welfare and the support of others, including me.

During his travels in Africa, Gordon married a woman we never met. They had two daughters, Jenny and Rachel. Gordon left this family too, but returned to Africa later to retrieve the children when his wife died. He came back to North Vancouver, where he raised them, but never contacted his first family. His daughters Carol and Susan discovered where he was when they read a newspaper story about a boat he was building in his backyard. Backyard boat-building had also been a feature of their early lives with their father.

There are lots of stories about Gordon that are not in this telling. They may seep out later. In the last years of his life, when he was dying of cancer, he had surgery that gave him a little more time so that he could finish raising his two younger girls and see them settled into adulthood. My family, having lived quite separate lives for many years, also drew closer together. Gordon spent time at my house when his son, Bob, was building it. He came to my housewarming party, gifted me a rope fire-escape ladder that he'd made himself (and which thankfully I've never had to use), and sometimes sat in my back garden with Jack and Vera and me. From memory, he drew a map of Hochfeld and the house we lived in there. When he was confined to palliative care in North Vancouver and I couldn't ride in a car to visit him, I wrote him letters two or three times a week. I told him about myself, in the past and in the present, recounting stories he hadn't heard before. In his last phone call to me, he thanked me for the letters and the financial support I had given him and his family and said he wouldn't bother me anymore. He died a week later, on February 17, 1990. His children were all very upset. I was very sorry.

I think Gordon's life, though often harsh, suited him. Perhaps his independence and his love of travel were an inheritance from our father. Then again, perhaps if our father had been alive through our childhood, he would have provided Gordon with a strong role model, an example of devotion and self-discipline. I thought the army had taught Gordon some self-discipline, and educated him to a degree, but still—and again—I was surprised when he appeared to be leading a conventionally responsible family life during his first marriage. When he crashed out of that life, I was extremely distressed and heavy-hearted, but I also recognized the brother who would not obey rules.

APPLES, ETCETERA

AFTER THE DEBUT of *Home Environment* at the Douglas Gallery, Ann Rosenberg, a critic and curator who later became a good friend, told me that my installation was very good, very strong, but not beautiful. Glenn Lewis's ceramics exhibition, which had previously been featured in that space, was beautiful, she insisted, but not mine. I thought, "Beautiful? I'll show you beautiful!" And I did—I created the *Fruit Piles*. Of all my ceramic sculptures, the piles of ceramic apples and oranges and grapefruit have been the most widely admired for their jewel-like colours, lustrous glazes, and gorgeous shapes—their beauty.

I had experimented with making ceramic apples and glazing them before I finished *Home Environment*. At some point, though, I had noticed a pyramid of apples at a corner grocer's and knew immediately that I could make something very special out of that everyday arrangement—sculpture that was part organic form, part geometric structure. Apples became my new joy: throwing

Some of my early ceramic fruit piles exhibited along with my later bronze snowballs in a survey show at the Equinox Gallery, 2015.

them on the wheel and then shaping them and piling them in pyramids—some of the pyramids with square bases and others rectangular—glazing them, and then firing them so that the glaze fused the apples together. I made more than two dozen *Fruit Piles* of different sizes, numbers, and varieties. The apples could be glazed bright or dark red—ripe or rotten. I also made glossy orange oranges and shiny yellow grapefruit, creating texture on the surfaces of the citrus fruit by rolling them on a screen door. Nothing was made in a mould; every individual piece of fruit was slightly different from the others, and each one, with its subtle bumps and undulations, bore the mark of my hand. I often thought of the ceramic surface as being like skin. The fruit were fleshy, sexy.

I exhibited a roomful of *Fruit Piles*, along with smaller sculptural tableaux, ceramic versions of still-life arrangements that related to my studies and that I called *Art School Teaching Aids*, as part of a two-person show, *29 Pieces*, at the Vancouver Art Gallery in 1970. Curator Glenn Allison did a glorious job of installing my work along with some of Glenn Lewis's wonderful porcelain sculptures on plinths. Apples, of course, are loaded with symbolism: sexuality, fertility, sin, redemption, delight. My shiny red apples seemed to delight people, but they also brought out the element of temptation, as did the other fruit.

A few years after the show, a neighbour was visiting me, a man I didn't know very well. One of my big pyramids of apples was sitting in my living room. He looked it over, uneasily, and then said, "I have something like that." I said, "You do? What is it?" A bit hesitantly he told me he thought it was a sculpture of cherries. Totally intrigued, I walked across the back lane to his place with him to look at it. Definitely not cherries. Definitely apples. Apples I had made. With a little thought, I recalled that, some years earlier, the Alma Mater Society at the University of British Columbia had acquired one of my *Fruit Piles* and that it had been stolen while being installed for an exhibition in the small gallery at the Student Union Building on campus. This happened, I believe, when the curator working on the show went for lunch or coffee or perhaps for a washroom break, leaving the gallery briefly unattended. My neighbour's sculpture was, I was certain, that purloined sculpture. He seemed to know nothing about that.

After I left, my neighbour contacted UBC and found out that the Alma Mater Society had collected insurance money for the lost art. The Society didn't want the original sculpture back. Nobody knew how many times it had changed hands or who the thief was. My neighbour and I could come up with no better plan than to leave it where it was. He had, after all, paid for it.

Another theft of my ceramic fruit occurred some years later. On my porch, I kept some artworks that were not saleable because the clay had been bad and, during the firing, produced little explosions all over the surface. The sculptures weren't blown to bits— nothing that dramatic—but they were covered in tiny pockmarks. I put a few of my damaged *Fruit Piles* on my porch, which was a lovely place to sit when the sun was out. I often ate my lunch or drank my afternoon coffee there, and I shared the space with my visitors too. We all enjoyed the presence of the pyramids of fruit, however imperfect they were.

One morning, I discovered that two of my pockmarked piles of fruit were missing. I was dismayed to lose an important part of the happy and comfortable outdoor environment that was my back porch, but I didn't report the theft. I didn't see the point. A few years went by, and then one morning when I let my little dog out, there were the two missing *Fruit Piles* sitting in my yard, a bit the worse for wear, a bit damaged in places. I was too stunned to question the blessing of their reappearance, but quickly got them, my brood, into the house. I cleaned them, repaired the broken parts, and put them back out on the porch, chained this time. Finding the culprit did not cross my mind.

Many more years later, I was at a luncheon honouring Adrienne Clarkson, who was Canada's governor general at the time. The master of ceremonies was the well-known Vancouver actress Nicola Cavendish. She was very funny—a true comedienne—and did a good job of introducing guests. At one point, she wandered off into a spontaneous story of her own—a story that turned out to be a public confession. She told us that when she was a second-year student at UBC and very poor, she had passed by a house with gorgeous ceramic fruit piles sitting on the porch. They were magnificent, she said. She'd never seen anything like them. She came back at night and took two of them home, where she enjoyed them for a while, promising herself that they were only a "loan." Here, our recollections of what motivated her to return them and when somewhat diverge, but return them she did—as she had taken them, in the dead of night.

Having related this story, Nicola asked my pardon in front of that large crowd. Then she got off the podium, found me at my table, bent down, and asked my forgiveness personally. It was very funny. She wanted to redress her crime by bringing me fruit, real fruit, from her parents' orchard. We discussed what that compensation might be. Apples? Hmm, no, not apples. "How about cherries?" I said, and then amended that. "No, cherry time is over. Maybe peaches."

Eventually, there were peaches at my front door.

Standing in my mother's garden in front of the little house—dark red with white trim—that we rented in North Kildonan, 1941. I am not showing off our home, however, but the sailor-style pantsuit I purchased with money I earned picking strawberries on a farm on the Red River.

MY HOMES

AND

HABITATIONS

MY FIRST MEMORY is of moving day in Hochfeld, where we lived for a few years after my father died. We arrived at what would be our home with a wagon full of possessions. I vividly recollect the loaded wagon behind me, and then walking into the house carrying a blue box and setting it down in front of a white Russian oven. I've repeated this story many times, and many times writers and curators have found echoes of this simple act in my later performance art. Hmm. I was two years old.

The house was built in the manner of old Mennonite houses in Russia, that is, with a covered passageway between the back door and the barn. This feature enabled a wagon to be loaded or unloaded while remaining sheltered from snow or rain. The whitewashed oven was also a traditional Russian design, simple but efficient. It was built of handmade bricks and used for cooking and for heating the house. There was a small, warm bench beside the oven, where my brothers slept. My mother and I shared a bigger bed. In summers, when it was hot, cooking took place outdoors. Others may have used wood for fuel, but mostly I remember that we burned dried cow dung.

Hochfeld was one of many small Mennonite farm-villages in southern Manitoba, and, like the houses and barns, it was also constructed on a traditional plan, in keeping with Russian Mennonite beliefs. The villagers willingly shared the land they had been allotted as homesteaders, and lived in a tightly knit way that preserved their sense of community, along with their language and culture. Many of the people in Hochfeld had come to Canada some fifty years earlier, although there were also more recent arrivals who had left Russia, as my parents had, in the 1920s. There was a long central street with narrow plots running back from either side of it. Each family had one of these plots, where they built their house and barn, planted their garden, and kept their cattle at night. Beyond that, there were larger parcels of land, where families pastured their livestock during the day and raised their crops. I don't remember any wheat being harvested. I expect there was hay. Certainly, there were haylofts.

Gordon and I would walk to the end of the village and look at the cows, which were grazing in the communal summer pasture or drinking at the waterhole that the farmers had dug for them. I remember the road lined with houses and an angry dog in one yard that caused me a lot of anxiety. Sometimes we stopped at a neighbour's house and were given paper cones of cherries, picked for us from their tree.

I have many other memories of Hochfeld, and some of them have found their way into my art. The watermelon fields in the heat of the summer. Taking a watermelon and breaking it over my knee, the sticky juice running down my legs and arms. The stickiness was uncomfortable, but the watermelons tasted so good and were so red. I remember, too, yelling and screaming, furious at having to take an afternoon nap, and then waking up, nap over, and being given an egg, which I could take to the store of our kindly next-door neighbours and trade for candy. That was my daily routine: nap noisily resisted, then waking up and carrying an egg next door. The egg was a precious thing in my hand. I held it preciously.

When we moved to Reesor, my first impression was how much *green stuff* there was after the dry prairies and the poplar trees of Hochfeld. How many evergreens there were, and how much moss. My stepfather's house, like most of the houses in Reesor, was built of logs. All the girls and the youngest boy slept in a bedroom on the main floor, the parents slept in the living room, and the other boys slept upstairs, which was a recent addition.

There were games in the woods during the summer, playing house, taking up great chunks of soft moss and settling them into forms like sofas and chairs. The roads were lined with raspberry canes, and near the schoolyard were wild strawberries that we picked in June. Later in the season, there were cranberries, and we picked buckets and buckets of them too—although you had to be careful where you stepped or you could sink forever into a bog. In the house in Reesor, there were also Christmas celebrations, of a kind my brothers and I had never experienced before. As winter came on, I heard rumours of Santa Claus, an entity entirely unknown to me. The rumours sounded magical, and set me up for shivery visions of wondrous possibilities. On Christmas morning, we awoke to a soup plate each, full of nuts and other treats: a few candies, an apple, and an orange. For the first time, there were gifts—paintboxes and colouring books. At our second Christmas in Reesor, my stepsisters Tina and Mary were given a beautiful old porcelain doll that had been their mother's and that had been wonderfully restored. I received a new, celluloid doll—a boy doll, which was a bit odd. I was happy enough to have it, but I couldn't help looking enviously at my stepsisters' far lovelier gift.

In 1935, when we arrived, penniless, in Winnipeg, we stayed for a brief period with my father's relatives, the DeFehrs, my mother and Gordon and I sharing one small room. Then we moved into a duplex in North Kildonan, a neighbourhood just north of Winnipeg that was recently settled by Mennonite farmers, who were also supposed to have access to work in the city. During most of my growing up, it was a "rural municipality" on the city's northern outskirts, although like East and West Kildonan, it would eventually be absorbed into the city of Winnipeg. The area where we lived resembled any other poor suburb, with small houses on earthen streets (later paved). The streets ran off the highway, on the other side of which were large market gardens, mostly owned by well-to-do Dutch farmers. Beyond the market gardens was the Red River, where wealthy people lived.

The duplex owned by the DeFehrs had been converted out of an old chicken house. It was a long building with a wall down the middle. Our side of the duplex had a big living room, a small bedroom, and a kitchen, and we shared these living quarters with a young, newlywed couple. Mother and Gordon and I occupied the bedroom—Jack was still in Reesor working to pay off our debt— and my mother did our cooking in the kitchen, where the bride also cooked. When Jack arrived in the spring, he had to sleep in the living room, where the young couple slept. It was not a happy arrangement. In the summer, we all moved out. My mother went to work on a farm at Domain, a hamlet about twenty miles south of Winnipeg, where I later joined her. Gordon worked on another farm, and Jack worked on a different farm, still.

When we came back together in Winnipeg, we spent a little time in a friend's small apartment, then landed in another unsuitable place for about a week, and finally moved in with another Mennonite family, the Spensts. There, we rented the living room and the tiny space next to it that led to the front door. Three of us slept in the living room, and one of my brothers slept in that little anteroom. The Spensts, who had a lot of children, lived in the rest of the house.

That was the winter I was bedridden for months, first with whooping cough and then with a long, undiagnosed illness. The four of us were packed into the one room with the stove, and my mother yelled at my brother and my brother argued back at her. It was not a salubrious environment in which to recover. When I stopped eating, my mother put a bowl of sugar in front of me and said, "Eat! Eat!" I didn't want sugar. I lay in bed with my face turned towards the wall. My mother was certain that I was going to die. Eventually, Mr. and Mrs. Spenst must have said something like, "Look, if you keep yelling, she's never going to get well." Suddenly, there was silence. The atmosphere became more like an infirmary than a battle zone. I started eating again and slowly regained my strength. I remember my first bath after my long illness. My ribs were sticking out, and the skin over them was blue and green. When I got up, I was too weak to walk. All I wanted to be able to do was dust the chairs. That was my greatest aim, to go from one chair to the next and dust.

When we moved out that summer, my mother and I did a lot of berry picking. We repaid the Spensts the money we owed for rent and got all our debts in order. By that time, we were able to move into a three-room house in North Kildonan. It was very small and it had an outdoor toilet, but it was neat and tidy and, oh, the luxury—we had it all to ourselves. The shingled exterior was painted dark red with white trim. At the back and side of the house was a large vegetable garden, where we grew carrots, beets, peas, potatoes, and cabbage. In the front yard, my mother cultivated a fancy flower garden. There was a centre circle and four triangles around that, all lined with white-washed stones, and white stones also lined the walk from the street and around the side of the house. My mother planted flowers within the circle and in the triangles in each of the four corners of the plot. We had plants in the house too, and one or two pictures. The floors were painted bluish-grey.

Every few years, we repapered the walls in the living room. Our landlord, who seemed to like us as tenants, supplied the paper, usually in subdued colours, tans and creams, with faint patterns. I had no idea anything brighter or more colourful might be available but, in fact, plain and understated suited us. Initially, my mother was in charge of hanging the wallpaper—and the results were horrifying. I was twelve or thirteen, and my job at first was to stand at the top of the ladder while also trying to secure the end of the paper. We measured and cut a piece and brushed paste on it. Corners and even whole swatches got stuck to the furniture on the way to the wall. Words were exchanged; tears were shed. On the second attempt, my mother took the top end of the paper to the top of the ladder while I held the bottom end steady. Her aim cannot have been true because the paper ended up at a crazy angle with folds in it, which meant removing the whole detestable thing and pasting it again. The double wetness made it mushier and harder to keep in one piece. In the midst of all this wrangling, I ended up stuck between the wall and the wet paper, as if in a slapstick comedy. Eventually it occurred to me that my mother could cook and sew, but she could not hang wallpaper. I cut her loose.

She was sure I couldn't manage the job myself, but I did. I measured a piece of paper, cut it, and applied paste to it, and then holding it carefully, got up on the ladder with it, letting the paper hang slightly out from the wall, and aligned it perpendicularly. When it looked right, I pressed it to the wall from the top to the bottom and from the centre to the sides. Yay! I could get the job done by myself, and in hours, not days. I went up several notches in my mother's estimation. Previously, she had thought I was clumsy.

I think my paper-hanging success had to do with a steady hand, a good eye, and tenacity. Mostly tenacity. But recalling those experiences now, I wonder if they created an aversion in me, a dislike in my artmaking, for sticking things to walls. I screen-printed wallpaper for my early installation *Home Environment*, but in its first incarnation, the wallpaper was pinned, not glued. In some of my later works—*Shirting*, a series of striped paintings on long vertical pieces of vellum, and *Crossed Ankles*, a large grid of many, many black-and-white photographs, also on vellum—I preferred to pin the tops of each sheet to the wall and allow the rest to hang freely so that the vellum fluttered gently as people walked by. Something in that movement appeals to me—the unstickiness of it.

After the war, when Gordon was working near an import business in Winnipeg, he brought home wooden packing crates, which smelled of tea. There were huge crates and smaller ones, all treasured by a family that would move house about once every year and a half for the next sixteen years. We first used those crates in 1946 when we moved to British Columbia, my mother and I staying for a while in Yarrow, then settling—more or less—in Chilliwack. Gordon and his wife Edith carried on to Vancouver. We moved three times in Chilliwack, our first abode being a small room on the second floor of a rooming house. The bathroom was on the first floor and was shared by the whole house. If you lived on the second floor, you got to the bathroom by walking to the end of the hall, pulling up a trap door, and climbing down a ladder, locking the trap door after you. Sometimes, when you opened the trap door, the bathroom was already in use by someone who had forgotten to lock it. These encounters were embarrassing—no, they were horrifying—to my eighteen-year-old person.

A few months into our tenancy, we moved to a slightly bigger room on the same floor. We had brought furniture from Winnipeg and were faced with the prospect of squeezing my mother's bed, a long couch, and many large crates into the single room in which we lived, cooked, ate, and slept. Meanwhile, across the hall there was much coming and going, knocking, shouting, swearing, and general unruliness and incompatibility. Two women were earning their living entertaining customers who were frequently drunk. I slept very little. In midwinter, church friends offered us a room with a semi-bathroom and an outside entrance. This place was a gem, and we quickly relocated there.

After eight months in Chilliwack, my mother and I finally moved to Vancouver to be closer to my brothers and their families. We rented two rooms in a house on 25th Avenue, near Fraser Street. After I had worked in the luggage factory for a couple of years and was generating a steady income, I borrowed money from a woman in our church—a woman who earned her living cleaning houses and who loaned us her savings—and made a down payment on a house on 31st Avenue, between Fraser and Main Streets. Of course, I paid her back promptly.

Ours was an old wooden two-storey house in a working-class neighbourhood. My mother's cousins, Helen and Renate, lived upstairs, and we occupied the main floor, which had a living room, dining room, large kitchen, and two small bedrooms. We shared the bathroom with our cousins. Apart from that inconvenience, it was lovely to get to know them and fascinating to hear their stories. They had managed to get to Germany from Russia during the war, and after the war, immigrated to Canada. They hadn't known my mother in Russia, but they knew of my father. Everybody in that old Mennonite community knew about my father, because of his musicianship and his work as a choral conductor. They thought the world of him.

When I found my first teaching job, I sold the house and bought a used car, and we moved to Surrey. The place we rented was unmemorable, and in some ways, renting instead of owning seems like a backwards move. However, I got good use out of the car, driving to and from work, taking singing lessons in Vancouver, singing in a choir in Abbotsford, and singing in another choir in Surrey.

With my second and longer-lasting teaching job, in Burnaby, I returned to Vancouver with my mother, and we lived in a succession of rented apartments and houses, including on one floor in Helen and Renate's house. We had become good friends, and since they had lived with us on 31st Avenue, it seemed natural that, later, we would share their house on Elgin Street. But then my mother became more and more paranoid, angry, and delusional. At her insistence, we moved six times between 1954 and 1962, when I bought my second house, a modest wartime bungalow on 51st Avenue, again near Fraser. I borrowed money for the down payment from my good friend and fellow teacher Elizabeth Klassen and secured a mortgage through the financial arm of the BC Teachers' Federation.

When we moved to that house, I bought a new car for the first time, so that I could get to my teaching job in Burnaby. Jack insisted it should be a "regular" car that started without using a throttle and a choke. About a year later, one of my fellow teachers came into the staff lunchroom and said that she was going to cash out her pension fund and take a trip to Europe. I immediately thought, "I can do that too, and paint for a year." But I had just bought the house and the car and owed money on both. In less than three years, however, I had paid off the loans.

In 1965, after twelve years of teaching, I cashed out my pension fund, about $2,000, and took a year's leave of absence. I spent two months in Europe with Elizabeth, and then came home to paint and continue my ceramics studies at the University of British Columbia. At the end of the year, I still had money left over, and since I was making and selling pottery, I took the next year off too. Later, I taught night classes in ceramics at a community centre and later, still, taught in the Fine Arts Department at UBC. I never went back to teaching full-time.

My home became more important than ever. I painted in the basement and worked on my ceramics in the garage, firing pots in an electric kiln there. To economize, I rented out the main floor of the house and lived in the unfinished basement for a summer. At one point, I slept in the garage. Elizabeth, who was finishing her degree at UBC, rented my extra bedroom for three years. In 1967, Charmian Johnson and I built the big gas kiln, also in my garage. My life was by then entirely given over to art, and my home was made to accommodate it.

In 1970, a few years after my mother had moved into a nursing home, I sold my 51st Avenue house and bought a 1920s Craftsman-style house in Kitsilano. The neighbourhood was popular with students and hippies, and the twined scents of incense and marijuana wafted out of the surrounding old wooden houses. Although my property was small, it was just a couple of houses away from lovely little Tatlow Park and handy to UBC, where I was teaching part-time. I shared that house—American visitors described it as a "cottage," which surprised me—with my good friends Tom Graff and Elizabeth. Tom lived in the basement suite, and Elizabeth, upstairs. I had an improvised studio in the garage, which I was later able to tear down and remake as a purpose-built studio. Designed by another friend, Rob Mackenzie, it was a sleek Modernist design, very handsome, with corners and chimney painted in alternating blocks of deep blue and white.

I lived in the Kitsilano house through the next eighteen years of my rapidly blossoming art career—and through the first year of my nerve-racking marriage. It is sometimes difficult to believe how prolific I was in the 1970s and '80s, inventing, producing, and touring performance works, by myself and with Tom; creating many successful series of ceramic sculptures, which were exhibited across the country and in New York and Paris; winning important public commissions; and painting again, in an entirely new way.

BOOTCASES

AFTER I HAD COMPLETED some twenty-five *Fruit Piles*, I began making men's shoes in clay and exhibiting them in glass-fronted cabinets, which I called *Bootcases*. The idea for this series came to me after passing a shoe store on Fraser Street. In the window were shelves with men's shoes displayed on them. I found it an interesting image without consciously knowing why, just as I had found the pyramid of apples in the corner grocery store interesting. From the first time I had used shoes, in my 1968 workshop performance, I understood their homely power, their ability to symbolize human presence and also human enterprise—tasks undertaken, distances walked—in an unpretentious way.

One day, after seeing the display in the shoe-store window, I came across a wall-mounted tool case in a thrift shop I regularly visited. The case was seven or eight feet long, about three feet high and six inches deep. It had three glass-fronted doors, the interior was covered in green felt, and there were hooks for hanging

Installation view of *Single Right Men's Shoes*
at the Vancouver Art Gallery, 1985.

tools. The *Bootcases* were coming to life in my mind. Glenn Allison helped me carry the case home. I immediately pulled out the innards and proceeded to make shelves and build up the bottom to window height, using wood, filler, and glue. I painted the inside white and the outside a dark, warm grey. (Sadly, it has since been painted another, colder grey, after sustaining some damage while being shipped across Canada for an exhibition.)

But the shoes! The shoes! My friend Tom Graff had bought some neat zippered black boots for himself. I used them as models for the first nine boots I made and installed in the altered tool case. My method of working was to roll out clay like pastry dough (although I had not yet learned how to make pastry dough); cut the various parts with a sharp knife, starting with the heel and then the sole; attach them; and then shape the uppers. The shape of a shoe is extraordinarily complex, as I'm sure any cobbler could have told me. I had to learn for myself. I wanted the shoes and boots to look real but not super-real. I didn't want to make sentimental, falling-apart old boots, but I wanted them to look like they'd been worn a little, with a few creases over the toes.

For the *Bootcases*, I did not want to make pairs either. I established the theme of single right men's shoes and boots, which I mounted on shelves in glass-fronted cases, with the inside of the shoe facing outward. The inside, with its zippers and seams, is the emotional side of the shoe. The outside, which is displayed in shop windows, is the public and decorative side. The shoes in style then had thick platform soles and big, clunky heels. I wanted classic shoes, styles that would endure through time when the trendy ones flopped. And so I borrowed some from my friends to model mine on: Tom's boots, Glenn Allison's blue-and-white high-top running shoes, and Salmon Harris's brogues. For the other styles—including bluchers, spectators, and patent leather shoes—I looked to an old catalogue.

The first *Bootcase* had fallen into my lap and needed only a little adjusting and shaping. For another, I used an old medicine cabinet of my friend Elizabeth's. The rest of the cases were made to order by the artist Max Dean, who had built the marvellous shipping crates for our performance tour. I painted some cases, flocked others, and used varnish to which I had added dry pigment of various kinds. I painted most of the shoes too, sometimes in the colours associated with them and other times, in the same colours as the cases—fire-engine red, pumpkin orange, mossy green. In total, I made some twenty *Bootcases*. They were very popular, and ended up in public and private collections across the country.

I also made a row of different styles of men's boots and shoes in pairs, all glazed in dark red, the colour of dried blood. Inside the heel of each shoe, I glued a decal of a pink rose. Installed in a gallery, these pairs of shoes stand in a row on the floor, beginning at the wall and drifting at a slight angle into the room. The *Bootcases* were first shown, with the long line of paired shoes, at the Vancouver Art Gallery in 1973. They were later exhibited in Victoria, Toronto, and New York—and in a solo show called *Single Right Men's Shoes* at the Canadian Cultural Centre in Paris in 1974.

Elizabeth and I went to Paris for a month to install the show there and to worry about the best images for the poster. We attended the exhibition opening wearing ridiculous long dresses while all the other women—elegant *Parisiennes*—wore stylish pants and tight turtleneck sweaters, with discrete, expensive pendants. After the opening, there was food at the curator's apartment. Everyone talked in French and we were a bit lost. The curator, however, spoke English. I told him how impressed I was that he and his team had handled my *Bootcases* as if they were as precious as Renaissance art. "But of course," he said, "your work is every bit as good as that." As good as Michelangelo, he added. Naturally, I liked him a lot.

The *Bootcases* travelled widely, and also showed up in my first retrospective exhibition at the Vancouver Art Gallery in 1985. They appeared, too, in my second retrospective exhibition at the Vancouver Art Gallery, in 2000, and at the National Gallery of Canada, when the retrospective toured. And, again, in a big survey show of my work called *The Things in My Head*, which the Equinox Gallery organized in late 2015.

Although hardly anything sold from my *Living Room Environment* show, my *Fruit Piles* and *Bootcases* really seemed to appeal to people. I was beginning to enjoy seeing my work displayed and celebrated in a number of public galleries. I was also gratified to be able to support myself with my art.

The Mennonite girls' club I belonged to in 1944.
I am the slightly out-of-focus girl seated at the
far right, and our club leader, Mia DeFehr, is
standing in the second row, second from the
left. My rebellious phase was over, but I was still
keeping secrets from my mother.

MY

SECRETS

WHEN CHILDREN BECOME teenagers, their parents are usually
appalled at what they have brought into the world. My mother
was fortunate in missing out on the rebellious phase of my ado-
lescence, not because I didn't turn into a monster, but because
I didn't direct my monstrous behaviour towards her. I felt sorry
for her and wanted to protect her, from the time she left her second marriage and we arrived in Winnipeg. I shared a bed with
her when I was young, and felt it shaking as she wept into her
pillow every night. I heard her cry during our evening prayers. I
felt sorry, too, for the many unhappy experiences she had when
members of our community condemned her for not staying with
her abusive husband. They also condemned her for my brothers'
wayward behaviour and their lack of commitment to our church.

Because I was careful not to hurt her and because I talked very
little to her about my experiences outside the home, my mother
never heard about my own naughty ways. Our conversations were

pretty mild and mundane, discussing subjects like sewing lessons, cooking, and berry picking. The most meaningful conversations we had were of her memories of life in Russia—but then, she did all the talking. I believe she told me all she could remember of those times because I asked about them over and over again. It wasn't easy for me to discuss my private fears and hurts with my mother, knowing that she was daily overwhelmed by hers.

My teenage rebellion took place primarily at school and during after-school activities. There was a strong element of performance in my acting out. In grade six, my best friend, Minnie, and I talked our mothers into making us identical dresses that were not exactly age-appropriate. Oddly, my mother and Mrs. Sawatzky seemed to enjoy seeing their daughters looking swanky. Minnie and I also acquired identical dark turquoise hats, broad-brimmed with veils spotted in hot pink. The veils made seeing difficult. We were often laughed at in public conveyances. We didn't care.

We played hooky too, not because we didn't like school—we did—but because it was daring and illegal and adventurous. Those were the days of truant officers who, if they caught you skipping school, could haul you back to class to face corporal punishment. We also tried to anger our teachers and interrupt lessons, to the amusement of our classmates. We forged our mothers' signatures on notes we wrote, excusing us from class. One day, having waited until we were good and late, we brought big pieces of rusted metal to class. We dragged the dirty rusted sheets up two flights of stairs and noisily dumped them at the back of the room, where students were supposed to leave scrap metal for the war effort. We were well aware that what we brought was of no use whatever. We got a huge laugh from the other students. Even our teacher could hardly keep her lips from twitching.

Another teacher used to walk up and down the classroom aisles as she talked and taught. I found this a perfect situation for attaching a clothespin to the bottom of her skirt as she passed by, unaware. When she discovered it, she was incensed and demanded to know who had done it. I put up my hand. Defiance and horridness were a part of me then, as was a brash compulsion to entertain.

Grade eight was the time of my worst rebelliousness, and it was directed at our long-suffering teacher, Mr. Wigmore. My reputation for bad behaviour had made me interesting to the other students. They were my friends, and they expected me to insert some drama into their day. I saw myself as an entertainer and felt obliged to disrupt the teaching in some stupid way, which often resulted in my being sent to the cloakroom. There I amused myself by reading a book about crime and insanity that had served for years to prop open the cloakroom window. I doubt anybody had ever read it. It was certainly beyond my comprehension. At one point when I was sent out of the classroom because of some transgression, I took the book with me and sat reading it on a piano bench in the main hallway downstairs. The principal walked by and asked what I was studying. I was greatly pleased to show him. He said it was a perfect fit. After that, I didn't need the book as a prop anymore.

Mr. Wigmore was a good soul and an excellent teacher, especially of history. He often threatened to report my bad behaviour to my mother, which secretly unnerved me. My one fear was that my mother would find out about my delinquency. Luckily he was too kind to let her know what I was up to. Nor did he ever send me to the principal for discipline. Perhaps the reason was that, despite all my unruliness, I excelled as a student. I found a way of learning material while I sat in the cloakroom. At night I crammed for tests. My friend Cornelius and I got the top marks in the class. It must have been difficult for my teachers. Later I regretted missing Mr. Wigmore's lessons in British history. They were much more interesting and thorough than the textbooks. But what could I do? I had a reputation to keep up.

Another strange thing happened during my rebellious phase. As a child, I had been mortally afraid of falling between the ties of the railway bridge over the Red River during expeditions to Kildonan Park with my friends and brother Gordon. In contrast, as an adolescent my fears of crossing that bridge evaporated. I loved to show off my agility and my apparent courage by walking on the railway ties on the outer edges of the bridge. I also used to walk on the railing of a highway overpass. Drivers would get out of their cars and yell at me and Minnie, my accomplice, to get down. I ignored them. Before each of these foolhardy adventures, I would ask myself, "Will it hurt me? Will it kill me?" I answered myself, "It may kill me, or I might only break a leg." Neither prospect stopped me.

Even now, this behaviour puzzles me. It wasn't courage, nor was it a desire to die. I loved life. And I was not, on the surface, a sullen teenager. I maintained a happy, easygoing exterior, especially at home or under pressure from authorities. That, too, might have been an act of defiance. At some point, the principal found a reason to strap me, and he seemed determined to punish me for all my past misdemeanours at the same time. He did his best to inflict pain—and he succeeded. I remained stubbornly cool during the strapping and thanked him when it was over. I knew I deserved it. My hands were excruciatingly sore for days. I couldn't sleep for the pain. Still, it seemed necessary to act as though it were nothing. My peers admired me for this bravado, but the most important thing was that my mother never found out. That would have been an unbearable punishment.

During the summer months between grades eight and nine, I decided that being bad was boring. All that time spent in the cloakroom was tedious, and I was missing out on a lot of things I was truly interested in. Grade nine was a clean slate. I liked my homeroom teacher and she liked me. I took on a few leadership roles, directed classroom Shakespeare rehearsals, and sang as a soloist at various functions and gatherings. My biology teacher didn't seem to mind that I slept through his classes. My English teacher thought I could write, but said my sentences were appalling. She soon set me straight.

Although I no longer courted trouble, there were still plenty of things I kept from my mother. One afternoon when I was about thirteen, I dropped into the Hudson's Bay department store to read for a bit before I went home. Reading provided me with a place of refuge, and I was leaning against a counter immersed in *Gone with the Wind* when a man came up to me and asked about the book. He seemed genuinely interested in what I had to say, and I was happy to discuss the book with him. Then he asked me to go to a movie, and I, thinking of movies I'd seen in which the heroine goes sailing off on a delightful adventure with a stranger, agreed.

To my surprise, when we entered the theatre, we sat at the very back. The movie was already in full swing, and I was immediately taken up with it. Soon after, a hand settled on my knee—the first hand that had ever been interested in my knee or any other part of my leg. I shook it off. The hand returned, furtively, and I removed it again, still immersed in what was happening onscreen. The hand refused to stop and began moving up my leg. I got up and walked out of the theatre.

To my consternation, the man followed me. I walked more quickly, almost running. He kept up with me, panting, begging me not to tell anyone what had happened. He didn't know that telling would be the last thing I would do, given that I found the situation so humiliating. He offered me money. I refused it and hurried on. He followed along beside me, stuffed money into my coat pocket, and ran off in the other direction. My heart was pounding. I was disgusted, with him and with myself. And what was I to do with the money? I couldn't take it home. Near our house, I passed a wooded area, a patch of small poplars and underbrush, and hid the money in what I hoped would be a dry place.

I told no one about the groping, but I did tell Minnie about the money. She thought it was exciting. I began to think so too. Together, we planned a grand Saturday pleasure trip. We took the bus to the Sherbrook baths, had a glorious time splashing around in the swimming pool, and spent even more time luxuriating in the hot showers. We also bought a lot of chocolate bars, the pleasure of which palled after a very short time. Then we went home to our respective mothers for dinner. I guess the outing to the Sherbrook baths and the chocolate bars were the adventure I'd hoped to have with the stranger. It was not at all romantic. Nor was a slightly earlier experience with our next-door neighbour.

The bachelor living beside us had always been very friendly to me, waving as he passed by in his sports car. In my world, we greeted everyone—friends, neighbours, even strangers—with a friendly salutation. This was one of the rules of the Sunbeam Club, a Mennonite girls' group I belonged to. (It was not unlike Brownies, except that in Brownies you learned to knit, and in the Sunbeam Club you learned to sew.) One day, he came to the door and asked if I would come over later and clean his house. It was winter, and as we were short of firewood, I agreed. I didn't enjoy cleaning, but I knew how to do it; I'd been cleaning other people's homes as a way of earning money for our family. I slipped through a gap in the wire fence that separated our yards and arrived at the man's house, surprised that there were no cleaning supplies in evidence. He invited me into the living room, where there was a large, flat sofa, something like a chaise longue, upholstered at one end. He lay down on it and asked me to do the same. I did, even though it made me extremely uncomfortable. He told me that I had always been so nice to him. He thought we were good friends. I lay there stiffly, saying nothing, wondering what he could be thinking. We weren't friends.

Would I give him a kiss?

"No."

He spoke some more about my good qualities. He urged me again and again to kiss him. He didn't touch me, but he maintained a verbal siege on my affection. I could hardly bear to lie there beside him. I felt as if I were trapped in a nightmare. Somehow, I got myself up from the couch and to the door. Money was offered. I hadn't cleaned his house and I refused it. He pleaded again for a kiss. He would give me twenty-five cents for one. I refused. He upped his bribe: seventy-five cents. I would not kiss him. He gave me the money anyway. It had to look to my mother as if I had done the housework. I took the money and ran home.

My mother naturally wondered why so little time had passed. She wanted to know how the cleaning had gone. I said there was none. What had I done to earn all that money, she asked. "Nothing," I said. She knew something had happened but, again, I refused to tell her.

It was Saturday, and that was bath night. This ritual took place in a metal tub in front of the kitchen stove. In winter, it was easier gathering snow from the yard than carrying water in buckets from the community pump. The melted snow, heated in kettles on the stove, made for lovely soft bathwater too. I scrubbed myself thoroughly, and my mother washed and rinsed my hair, drying it with a rough towel. I welcomed this cleansing of my body and spirit, but it was accompanied by much scolding and suspicious demands to know what had happened next door. My mother never found out, but we used the seventy-five cents the neighbour gave me to buy firewood.

After that incident, I stopped calling out "Hello!" as the neighbour drove by. I tried to avoid looking in the direction of his house, and I never again approached the fence between our back gardens.

IN MIDDLE AGE, I recounted these childhood stories—and other later experiences with married men propositioning me, harassing me, and then begging me not to tell their wives—to some of my friends. My friend Elvira wanted to know why I was prey to these men. What was I communicating to them, consciously or unconsciously? I thought, "You had five sisters; you were never alone." I was frequently alone. And I put on a friendly face. Was it at the urging of our Sunbeam Club leader? Or was it my own form of camouflage, hiding my fears and worries and dark secrets from my mother and everyone else too?

As an old lady, I have no trouble smiling at strangers and saying hello. The lessons of the Sunbeam Club have taken a geriatric turn. But I sometimes think of my grade eight teacher Mr. Wigmore, poor man. For a long time, I wished that I might run into him and apologize for my beastly behaviour. I wished I could get my meanness off my conscience.

VENERATION

OF THE

WHITE COLLAR

WORKER

MY FIRST PUBLIC COMMISSION was a big challenge, but also very valuable to me early in my career. I had been a professional artist for only a few years when, in 1971, I was asked to submit ideas for two ceramic murals, each nine-and-a-half feet high by twenty-eight feet wide. The murals were to be installed in a new building being constructed for the Department of External Affairs in Ottawa. A colleague in Vancouver, Marguerite Pinney, was on the committee to choose an artist and had put my name forward. I believe she and others who supported my nomination for the job imagined I would do something luscious and beautiful, like my *Fruit Piles.*

I couldn't see fruit as being part of this commission at all. I thought and thought and came up with the idea of shirts—rows of shirt fronts, slightly undulating, with pockets and dark red ties. On one wall, subtly striped shirts, black on white, and on the other wall, coloured shirts, the panels of each mural arranged in a grid,

Standing in front of *Veneration of the White Collar Worker #1*, one of my two newly installed ceramic murals in Ottawa, 1974. Mounting it was a huge task that would have been impossible for me without the hard work of my friends Glenn Allison, Tom Graff, and Elizabeth Klassen.

three panels high and eight wide. The idea grew out of a drawing I had made for *Home Environment* and a subsequent series of tableaux of found and ceramic objects titled *Man Composition*.

At the time, it seemed to me that most of the people employed in that federal department were what were called "white collar workers." This was also a period in which I was focused on the symbolic possibilities of men's clothes, the presence and power they represented. (Some observers thought these works were about loss, about absence rather than presence.) After working out the recurring form, I submitted drawings and also charged ahead and made a sample component out of clay. It was a section of a man's shirt front, showing the placket complete with buttons, the upside-down V-shape at the bottom of the shirt, and a handkerchief pocket. This prototype was big—thirty inches by forty inches—and I was not completely convinced I could fire it in one piece in my gas kiln, which was notoriously uneven in the heat it generated. Still, I tried, and sure enough, the shirt broke into hundreds of pieces. I suppose I should have known better because I had already tried to fire two different ceramic coats holus-bolus in the gas kiln and they broke too. I had been overly optimistic, hoping that the shirt would be a blessed exception. Dreamers must have their dreams.

By the time I received my first funds for the commission, however, I had worked out a practical plan. I fashioned the clay into rectangular shirt fronts, each thirty inches high by forty inches wide and about two-and-a-half inches thick, one at a time, and then carefully cut each rectangular panel into six parts, three across and two down. On sunny days, I lugged these heavy pieces of clay out into my yard to dry, and then brought them into my studio for the night. Eventually, all the necessary hundreds of components were made, dried, and fired in my electric kiln. Then I assembled the pieces for each individual shirt panel and glued them onto three-quarter-inch plywood. I filled the joints with a glue-paste (my own recipe of filler, glue, and water, an amazingly strong mixture that dries as hard as fired ceramic) and used an electric sander to hide all traces of the cuts I'd made. It was an enormous and seemingly interminable amount of work, making, drying, cutting, and firing the panels; assembling and gluing them together; sanding them; painting them; lugging the heavy things back and forth, between my yard, my garage-studio, and my house, in various stages of completion. Elizabeth, who is as small as I am, helped me carry these heavy objects, weighing more than fifty pounds each, around the crowded basement.

I was pleased to make friends with the owner of a nearby lumberyard, who offered to find and deliver a large number of gallon-cans of glue to Ottawa for the installation of the murals. More help arrived in the form of my friend Tom Graff's parents who were visiting him during the summer. His father, an engineer, took a keen interest in my large folly. Later, when he had returned home, he designed and cut a wooden template so that I could accurately measure and make holes on the back of each shirt, for mounting. He also made, by hand, one hundred steel pins to hold the shirts firmly to the wall. What an invaluable friend he was! At Christmas, he and his wife visited again and he handed over the steel pins—as precious as gold nuggets.

The ties, which I made separately, to be glued on once the panels had arrived safely in Ottawa, were to be red, of slightly varying lengths and hues. The white shirts were to have fine black lines running across them, to give them a somewhat three-dimensional quality. To achieve this effect, I had to draw hundreds and perhaps thousands of straight lines, using a ruler, no mistakes, across the uneven ceramic surface. I must have been either brave or crazy—or both. To my surprise, I discovered it could be done. To my horror, the lines faded within days because I had drawn them with a felt-tip pen. I solved that problem by investing in permanent ink, which I applied with a steel-tip pen. The miracle of somehow not making big black blobs on the wavy surface of the clay or of not swerving off into space with the always-wobbly ruler never ceased to amaze me. It still amazes me. The fine black lines ran in neat parallels while also following the slightly undulating surface of the shirt fronts, creating an understated aesthetic.

The second mural was to reflect office workers' taste in fashion at the time, which was for coloured shirts. My options seemed wide open, but it was not to be so. I wanted the shirts to be green, shading from pale green to very deep green, almost black. When I suggested this palette to a designer in the architectural firm I was working with, she strongly impressed on me that the shirts should not and could not be green. She had already chosen and ordered hand-woven curtains with blues and purples, and my mural would have to fit into this colour scheme.

I was irked. It was a bit like being told that your painting has to match someone's sofa. However, unable to change the situation, I chose blue for the second mural. While blue was then a popular colour for shirts worn by businessmen, it had a long-established and entirely different meaning from white. "Blue collar workers" denoted people working in industry, which meant mixing my metaphors. Still, on we went. In the dry middle of the summer, no threat of rain, we put all the panels that were to be blue on the back lawn and laid them out in a grid, in the order they would take on the wall. I had purchased cans of blue, black, and white enamel paint, and mixed the brightest blue colour for the middle panel. By adding certain small amounts of white paint to the blue, I could make an even gradation of light blue to bright blue through the first half of the mural. Similarly, I added measured amounts of black for the panels in the middle and lowest rows, arriving at a dark, rich midnight blue—almost black—by the last panel. I hired my friends Glenn Allison and Salmon Harris to do the painting. Both of them were appalled by the simplicity of my method of pigmentation, but they followed my orders and found that my calculations had been right.

Glenn and Salmon also applied the final coat of polyester resin to the shirts, creating a permanent and glossy finish. With Tom and Tom's parents, Glenn, Salmon, and Elizabeth, we celebrated the completion of this seemingly interminable and at times almost impossible task. As with so many occasions in my life, our celebration took the form of a meal. In this instance, it was a delicious lunch in the backyard, accompanied by apple cider. Apple cider of the alcoholic variety, a rare indulgence. Elizabeth became quite tiddly and couldn't stop giggling. I myself suffered no pain. We were all of us flying high.

My shirts were ready to be installed well ahead of time and hunkered in big piles in the basement for almost a year before the building welcomed them in. I shipped them by truck to Ottawa, but foolishly, made no demands that the truck be heated while the shirts travelled across the frozen Prairies. I had thought that fired clay would be impervious to changes in weather and temperature, but within a year, the resin finish cracked, producing fine lines all over the surface of each shirt. Happily, I could repair this problem later by applying another layer of polyester resin to them.

For the installation in Ottawa, which took a couple of weeks, we were a team of four—Elizabeth, Tom, Glenn, and I—and with the exception of Glenn, we were all short. Glenn was taller, but thin. We didn't look big or strong enough to mount the large, heavy, cumbersome panels on the wall. We surprised everyone—even ourselves. Nevertheless, the work was exhausting. Every morning, we took our aching bodies to the cafeteria to power ourselves up for another day. There were high pot lights in the eating area, shining—no, glaring!—straight down on our heads, casting our faces in shadow. The shadow did nothing admirable to our haggard features. We looked at each other with dismay while we ate.

At the External Affairs building, we unpacked the shirts and placed them flat on the floor in their correct order. While the other three measured out the placement of the mural components, I glued the dark red ties to the striped white shirts. The bullet-like steel pins that Tom's father had made for us held the shirt panels in place on the wall while the glue that needed to further secure them to the wall was drying. The wooden template he had made showed us where to drill holes in the back of each panel and in the walls. My team and I mapped out the two walls with red ochre lines, making twenty-four equal-size spaces on each wall, and allowing for half-inch borders around them for grouting. Our measuring devices were old-fashioned but dependable: a plumb line, measuring tape, red ochre powder, and string. We dipped the string in the red ochre, held it in place top and bottom, and then pinged it in the middle, marking the wall in a straight line.

During this process, two of us stood on scaffolding and two of us, below. We were hard at work for a good while. When we turned around, we saw that the construction crew, still completing the interior of the building, were standing behind us, silently watching. They had gathered to see how four small people accomplish the kind of big job that they, the burly workers, usually do. They said nothing, but we sensed that they were impressed with us. Luckily, nobody dropped the powder line or screwed up the measurements.

After that, the crew came around to watch the heavy lifting too. Two of us at ground level prepared each shirt by inserting the steel pins into the holes we had drilled using the template and then covering the back of each shirt with my recipe of glue, wood filler, and water. Then we would hoist the prepared shirt up to the two standing above on the scaffold. Carefully, the pins in the shirts were directed into the corresponding holes in the wall. Each successful lodging of a shirt, not crooked, not lifting anywhere, was like a ringing score for the little Vancouver-ites. Getting all the shirts up, not crooked, not lifting anywhere, required forty-eight scores, no misses, no fumbles. I admit that every morning I held my breath until I saw the murals again. I had the awful apprehension that something might have fallen off the walls during the night. What then?

Mounting the shirts on the walls was not the end of the process. The spaces between them had to be filled. As grouting, we used the same glue-filler mixture as before, but thicker. Glenn sat on the floor measuring out the ingredients and kneading them into a thick paste. When the rest of us tried to apply the paste to the linear spaces between the shirts, it stuck to our hands and refused to lie flat. We kept working at it, but succeeded only in making a very rough and unkempt surface, and ending up with some paste on the ceramic shirt fronts, not to mention all over us. Finally, one of us had the idea of using the back of a metal spoon to make the paste lie flat and even. We borrowed four stainless-steel soup spoons, and they worked like a charm. The splodges of paste on the panels were removed with vinegar. We could see that there would be an end to our torturous work.

The construction workers were not the only audience to our labours. The cleaning women loved the goings-on. They came to admire the mural rather than check out our workmanship. Some of them asked me whether, if there were any extra ties, they could have them. There were extras. I gladly gave them the ties.

As we were nearing the end of the installation, I ordered more wood filler and other materials and arranged for late access to the building so we could work into the evening. The materials had been delivered to us, but I'd signed for them with sticky hands without checking to be sure the order was complete. Later, I discovered that the wood filler was missing. I phoned the provider who insouciantly said they were out of stock and so had not brought it. Our evening's work was in jeopardy.

One of the construction workers kindly offered to drive me to the store to demand the undelivered goods. There, I explained my problem and emphasized that I felt I'd been let down. I raised my voice. The employees argued back. I pounded my fists, and bits of dried glue and filler went flying. Just as we had reached the climax of our confrontation, a man who had quietly slipped out the back door of the shop reappeared bearing bags of the missing wood filler. I paid, thanked him, and left. The driver who had been so chatty on the way there was completely silent on the way back.

When the work was finally finished, we were called into the construction supervisor's office. He congratulated us in the warmest way for our labours and told us he would hire us anytime to work for him. Imagine our jubilation. We should have celebrated the successful end of the project, but we were much too tired to think about it. Tom took some photos of the finished murals and sent them to his father. Glenn went his own way. Elizabeth, Tom, and I visited friends and galleries in Toronto, Hamilton, and London, Ontario, before heading home.

WHEN I SAW the murals again several decades after we installed them, one of the ties was missing. By that time, I didn't know who was in charge or how to locate them. This damage troubled me for a very long time: one of my best works of art looked as though it had a tooth missing. Much later, one of the women in our church asked if there was anything she could do for me. Jo-Anne Stephens is a crack investigator; never lets go of a difficult undertaking, I had been told. I asked her to find out whom to contact to get the missing tooth fixed. She hunted down the people in charge of maintaining government-owned artworks, and they found the pieces of the broken tie and repaired it. I received a photo of the mural. The tie is in place, thanks to Jo-Anne and the people she contacted. Resolution happened in an unexpected way—one of those blessings that has filled my life.

The Problem With Wedding Veils,
2011, papier mâché and mixed media,
152.4 × 147.3 × 121.9 cm.

MY

MARRIAGE

I AM A PEACEMONGER at heart, although I sometimes manage to annoy my friends. I've been known to bring on volleys of anger, too, and even tears. Still, I was surprised at my friends' reaction when I told them I was going to be married. I was surprised, too, when my husband—before he reached that blessed state—asked me if he could have a car when he got out of jail. I thought he was being unusually solicitous. It never occurred to me that he would do anything other than find a job and earn the money to buy one for himself. Of course he could have a car!

I met Dwight in an unusual way. He was a prisoner in the provincial penitentiary in New Westminster and heard me being interviewed on a radio program. He wrote me a letter in early September 1973 and asked if I would write back to him. He mentioned that he had been reading Nietzsche. We corresponded for a few months, and then, in the spring, I began to visit him in jail. I was forty-six and he was twenty years younger. Previously I had made prison visits through an outreach program of the Vancouver Art Gallery, and I had also sung in prisons with direction from my church. I knew a little about the criminals I met, but I didn't know then how hard it is for someone who has been in jail most of his life to function outside of that environment.

After a few visits, Dwight asked me to marry him and I agreed. People have repeatedly asked me why I would marry a career criminal, and all I can say is that I loved him. He was handsome and charming and attentive. I didn't know what his history was or would be. Agreeing to marry him was probably not a rational decision, but once I'd made it, I stuck to it stubbornly. My friends were initially anxious for me. And then they were upset with me. And then they were angry at me. Only Elizabeth refrained from joining their chorus. She told me later that she knew I was a survivor and that I would get through it and be okay. She knew, too, that there was no point in arguing with me. I was not to be deflected.

We were married in my church in November 1974. Elizabeth made my wedding dress. By then, both she and Tom had moved out of the rental suites in my house and, with three other friends, into a big white house in Burnaby. When Dwight moved into my Kitsilano home, he painted the exterior brown, a colour I don't like, and remodelled the room that was to be his den. He also painted black borders around the fireplace and on a table in the living room, succeeding in making the place less mine than his. Eventually, it must have occurred to him that he should find work. He set off one day and came back much later, a cigarette dangling from his mouth. Before I let him kiss me, I pulled the cigarette out and flung it on the floor. There was no job. He appeared to do a few more days of searching, but I saw no evidence of success. Much later, after our marriage had broken down and he was in jail again, I asked him why he hadn't tried harder to find a job. He said that I made money so easily, without effort, so why should he work?

Given how hard I work, and how seriously, his response amazed me. Still, so many other people assume I have nothing but fun in my studio, that I suppose this is a common misapprehension. Let me be very clear: making art is not fun. The work is absorbing, and eventually, when it is completed, it might be gratifying. But it is not easy. It is not effortless. It is not *fun*.

Apart from the soon-apparent fact that I would have to support Dwight, the early weeks of our marriage were happy enough. He came to church with me, took part in things, met my friends, accompanied me to parties, and was there when I hosted parties in our home. It was only when I was alone with him that I began to realize how boring he was—how vacant. He didn't read (so much for Nietzsche), and if I was reading, even a newspaper, he thought I was pouting. He expected my total presence, my total focus, when we were together.

It took Dwight some time to find the car of his dreams. One day, he and a friend took me to view the prize he had set his heart on: a shiny, second-hand Corvette, the brilliant blue colour of a Steller's jay. It was not my kind of car—I thought it was a bit sleazy—but that's what he wanted. Now, how to pay for it? Dwight took me to a moneylender in New Westminster. The interest rate this man proposed was so exorbitant that it would have kept us in bondage for a very long time, perhaps forever. Dwight was not listening. Since I was the one with the income and the credit rating, why should he pay attention to the details of a loan from this man? In an attempt to bring him back to focus, I said, "All right, we'll take your offer." Dwight sat up and listened.

I made the moneylender go over the terms of the loan again and the interest he would charge and, for the first time, my husband actually heard what he was saying. His wits pricked up along with his ears. "We're not going to pay these ridiculous fees!" he said. "We're out of here!" Our next stop was my bank, which, on the strength of my assets and my sterling record of past loans made and repaid, lent us the money. The loan, of course, was in my name. I would be making the monthly payments.

That car gave Dwight a lot of joy. At that time, I had no idea that flashy cars were part of his criminal identity, his m.o. Nor did I know that another very particular car would play a role in convicting him of a violent crime. Dwight wanted me to be able to drive his Corvette occasionally and took me out to the deserted, weekend roads at the university to teach me how to operate it. I learned how, but never actually drove his car after that first lesson. I was happy with my own clunker. Cars are, for me, purely practical vehicles for getting from one place to another. I don't see them as status symbols. It is true that I will stop to look at a sleek and expensive car on the street, just as I would stop to look at a fine piece of design of any kind. I don't actually want to own it.

Before our first Christmas together, I had been asked to make a huge Advent wreath for our church. I wove together dark evergreen branches studded with brightly coloured straw flowers and roses and other lovely ornaments. There were long ribbons in rich, dark colours and large candles, which I fastened to the wreath. It was to be hung in the sanctuary of the Killarney Park Mennonite Church, but how to get it up there? I twisted Dwight's arm, and with less than good grace, he climbed a very tall ladder and installed it. His efforts were appreciated—and Christmas had begun. At home, there was a beautiful little tree, another Advent wreath, and other festive decorations.

Our yard was surrounded by a row of evergreens that I had dug out of a path on the way to Lake Cowichan, on Vancouver Island, many years earlier. They had grown against all odds (including being hit and wounded by the lawnmower on many occasions). By the time of my marriage, there was a tall, thick border of green trees around the yard, a gorgeous vision in the land of naked lawns. But was it Christmas Eve when I noticed that one of the nicest trees had been cut off close to the ground? It looked as if a tooth had disappeared from a formerly beautiful smile. Obviously someone had helped himself to a Christmas tree.

Dwight had been concerned that we should invite some poor soul from the penitentiary to our midday Christmas meal, but it was too late to make the arrangements. Instead, he brought an attractive hooker who made no waves but added a bright voice to the conversation. We didn't discuss her profession, but I no longer wondered about who had benefited from the gap in our row of evergreens. Dwight had obviously made a gift of it to her.

After our big lunch, Dwight took his friend home. Later, there was to be another festive meal at our house, with hordes of friends, a Santa Claus, and Christmas stockings for all. It was a lovely event to anticipate, except that there was a long wait for the Christmas stockings, which Tom was responsible for filling and delivering. He arrived with all the loot, and he, Elizabeth, our friend Jeremy Wilkins, and I set to work in the kitchen, stuffing stockings for at least twenty people. In the living room, the guests were restive. And where was Dwight?

Eventually, after the concerted preparations, Tom outfitted himself as a very credible Santa Claus with a big sack on his back. He came roaring into the living room, spreading cheer and gifts. Each person received a long stocking filled with a few nice little things plus candy and nuts, an apple, an orange, and finally an onion and some other vegetable with which to start a soup. It was great fun, and since we all lived modestly, we were filled with delight. Then we sat down to our evening meal and lots of laughter.

At some time during the festivities, Dwight arrived home, without the hooker, and resumed the role of The Husband. Something in his behaviour suggested he was jealous of Tom's success as Santa Claus. Maybe he was miffed that so much attention was focused on someone other than himself. For my part, I mourned the missing tree for years. At the time of its disappearance,

Dwight feigned sympathy. Later a new stem grew out of the old trunk, and eventually the gap was no longer visible.

In the new year, Dwight's friend Ron, who was recently released from the penitentiary, came to stay with us. Dwight was constantly checking the SPCA for forlorn animals, and one day he and Ron brought home a monkey in a large cage. My little dog, Lady—a grey toy poodle that was a gift from Dwight and that had been given up by her original owners—was immediately obsessed with it, standing on her hind legs, trying to make contact with the monkey and demonstrate her love and devotion. Because he was a rhesus monkey, we called him Reese.

Ron and Dwight took apart the heavy wire cage and fastened it to the front of a walk-in closet with a window, off the TV room. They placed a bar stool in the newly built cage and offered up numerous toys for Reese to play with, but he was not a bird, easily pleased. He threw the stool around and broke it, smashed the light bulb, and mangled the toys. The men then placed metal cages over the light and the window. I quickly saw something that Dwight did not, that Reese would need intense care and lots of attention. Not only that, but he shat and pissed so much that his cage needed daily cleaning.

Although Dwight wasn't working, I was—in preparation for a show at the Burnaby Art Gallery. I had taken a lot of time off in the fall, with a belated honeymoon and organizing a Christmas pageant at our church and entertaining Dwight's family when they visited. Glenn Allison, who was the curator and also living in our basement suite, talked to me seriously: the work had to be done in quick time to meet the deadline. No more fooling around.

Coincidentally or not, my new piece *Herd Two* had to do with animals: it was a group of galloping horses, the forms based not on actual horses but on the kind of painted ponies found on midway carousels, or singly, as a coin-operated ride for children in a supermarket. I cut twenty-four four-foot-long horses out of thick plywood, and made them look three-dimensional by drawing on them with soft lead pencils and erasers. Each horse was an individual: each head at a different angle; each coat differently shaded and patterned; each mane, tail, bridle, rein, and saddle carefully rendered. I was working as fast as I could, with a small dog draped around my neck like a fur collar, a screaming monkey in the other room, and Glenn's sister as a guest, as well as Ron. Art critics often read a state of panic in my herd of stampeding horses. Perhaps they are right.

I hoped I could be forgiven for telling Dwight that the dog was mine and the monkey was his. He would have to look after Reese and, for a while, he did that. However, he began to be away from the house for longer and longer periods of time each day, meeting old men friends and new women friends and accumulating speeding tickets. He often neglected to clean Reese's cage. A big, bad smell invaded the house.

As time went by and Dwight's attention was focused elsewhere, he often didn't come home at night. When his absences extended over three or four nights, I was furious, not only for the obvious reasons but also because he wasn't caring for Reese. One day, I suggested that since Dwight wasn't there to bathe the monkey and clean his cage, we would have to give him away. Reese, that is. Dwight looked surprised and a bit sullen. He mumbled some things I can't remember, but he made no commitment to being home every day. Reluctantly, we put ads in the paper for the monkey.

For a brief period, neighbours with two young children adopted Reese. When it became obvious they couldn't look after him adequately either, they returned him to us. Happily, a fellow in Alberta, who knew how to care for monkeys, contacted us and took Reese into his home. Dwight wasn't altogether chuffed, as he'd thought Reese was perfectly all right in our home. Although I was relieved, Reese's departure was not all joy for me either. I, too, am fond of animals, and Reese and I had formed a bond.

After Reese left us, Dwight cleaned out the cage and returned the room to its previous condition, more or less. Slowly the house lost its stinky zoo smell and recovered a state of equilibrium. Glenn's sister went back to her errant husband after he showed her a decent degree of remorse. Glenn moved out of the basement suite. Ron left us too. The house was pretty quiet for a while.

For my birthday, my friends Elizabeth, Tom, Elvira Wiebe, Alfred Siemens, and Jeremy Wilkins invited us to their house and served a delicious dinner: roast beef with all the trimmings. We sang together too. I knew that they regarded Dwight with deep suspicion, and he knew it too. He always felt a bit nervous among them, especially since they sang so well and discussed varied and interesting topics about which he had no concept. He had spent most of his life, even as a teenager, in some prison or other. Still, my friends were gracious and warm to him, and I suffered no unhappiness on behalf of my husband. After dinner, Dwight left to meet some of his friends, and I stayed overnight and enjoyed a relaxing morning with my friends.

Dwight picked me up, as promised, and took me home—and then went out again. When he returned, around midnight, he snuggled into bed, sighed, and told me he was glad to be home with me, safe and sound. I asked him what had happened. He told me that he and Ron had taken a trip out of town to commit a robbery. From what I could tell, the place seemed to be a pension-fund organization. Dwight said he hadn't known there were also going to be two professional gunmen from Quebec in on the heist. Ron didn't trust them and wanted Dwight to carry a gun, as his backup. In the end, however, Dwight's Corvette had got hung up on a snowbank, and he and Ron had had to beat a retreat before the heist occurred. Dwight said he was relieved. He didn't want to carry a gun. Too many things could go wrong.

Dwight's plans did, perhaps, affirm my friends' doubts about him, but all I could feel at the time was happiness and relief that he hadn't taken part in the robbery. I fervently wished he would never plan any such thing again. Yet somewhere inside my head there was the niggling thought that my husband would happily have carried out the heist if no guns had been involved.

Dwight had been draining our bank account, and there actually came a day when he could see that it was empty and he would have to find a job after all. He scanned the newspapers and saw an ad that appealed to him. A market gardener on Marine Drive needed help. The operation of big machines was a requisite of the work. Dwight had experience with heavy machinery, and he got the job. After he had worked for a week or so, his boss and wife invited me over for coffee. They were, indeed, good people. A large rock began to lift itself off my back. I thought Dwight would stop running around all day and all night and earn his own living. He wouldn't have much time to devote to his underworld friends. Did I really believe that? I'm not sure. Still, it seemed like a positive step—and it certainly aided our survival for a short time. Dwight loved coming home with a bag of groceries. At least he had paid for them himself.

One evening, he told me he was going to a meeting with his boss and other workers and wouldn't be home until late. It got to be midnight. I was getting angrier and angrier that an employee should be kept working so late and so long. I thought of phoning his boss and ranting at him, and then I *did* phone his boss and rant at him. I woke him up. "Meeting?" he asked. "What meeting?" I explained the story. He crossly hung up, but not before directing some words my way that I need not repeat here. I realized that Dwight was on another illegal mission. The next morning, when

I told him what I'd done, there was a note of awe in his voice: "You did? You phoned my boss at twelve o'clock at night?" Dwight never told me when his employment with the market farmer ended. Maybe it was the night I phoned the boss.

Dwight and I took turns getting up first in the morning and making breakfast. One morning he encouraged me to stay in bed a bit later than usual. After breakfast, he drove off in his Corvette, and I worked on another of the plywood horses. I was still at it when Dwight phoned to tell me to look out the back window. His voice sounded strangely uneasy. I looked. "Your car is back there, right?" I said, yes, it was. Something was up, but I didn't know what.

Later, while I was still working on my horses in the living room, two men visited me, policemen in plain clothes. We all sat down. One of them tried to make friends with my always-friendly dog. She growled. They asked me about Dwight's movements that day. I told them what I knew, which was nothing. At the beginning of our involvement with each other, when I recognized that Dwight was less than perfect, I told him that I would never lie for him. He'd grumbled about that, but I figured that if he did nothing illegal, I wouldn't have to lie. As the interview with the plainclothes men drew to its end and they left, one officer said, a bit bitterly, "You lied about one thing." I didn't know what, but I didn't challenge his remark. I may have omitted to mention Dwight's phone call. I knew my husband was in big trouble, but I still had no idea what he had done.

Sometime later, Dwight came home looking dishevelled and wearing someone else's clothes. He told me that he and some friends had tried to hold up a bank. They didn't quite manage to pull it off, and he expected to be picked up by the police pretty soon. I made dinner—fruit and cottage cheese—and we ate. The police arrived and took him away. He was gone for a day, and then phoned to ask me to fetch him. I did that. There were a number of cigarette burns on the back seat of my car. Somebody had obviously spent a lot of time there.

Things more or less returned to "normal" after Dwight's arrest except that he was away from home for longer and longer periods, giving me no clue where he was or why. Billy Lemon, another friend of Dwight's, was living with us, fresh out of prison. Billy always had his radio on, and one day I said, "Billy, all these songs are so sad. Why do you play such sad songs?" He said, "The songs aren't sad. You're sad."

There came a morning, in June, when Dwight got home after he'd been gone for days and Billy told him he had to tell me what was going on. I was still in bed. Dwight came upstairs to our bedroom and said he was sorry to sadden me, but he had been seeing his first wife for some time and wanted to continue to do so. There had been other liaisons, too, he confessed, including one with a bank teller, for whom he had set up a shared apartment. With my money, I supposed. This was a teller who worked at the credit union where I banked. I was crying and crying, sorrowing at what I saw as the end of our marriage. I had gone into this union expecting and believing that it would be a good one.

Dwight came up with a plan: he would continue seeing his former wife but would not leave me entirely. He would come and go, using the spare room downstairs. I said, "No—if you're leaving, you should leave for good." While my head was hanging down with grief and tears, I could feel an odd smile forming on my lips. The outrageousness of his suggestion! He wants to have both homes, I thought, ostensibly to comfort me but actually so that I would continue to provide bed and board for him between his adventures. "No," I said again. "You should leave entirely."

When Dwight left my house for good, after eight months of marriage, his car went with him. He had cleaned me out completely, and I had to teach in the Fine Arts Department at UBC to support myself again, and to replenish my resources. And I had to borrow money from Tom to make my mortgage payments that summer. I continued to pay off Dwight's car too, until, by accident, Glenn ran into him and told him he had to take over the payments because I had no money. Dwight was working then, in Powell River, where he was living with his first wife. He did take over the payments, but I was still registered as the car's owner.

The next fall, Dwight came by with a very sorry-looking vehicle. His Corvette appeared to have gone through a great deal of angry brush, and some of its parts were no longer firmly attached. Dwight wanted to trade in the car for an antique, a black 1936 Ford Business Coupe with curling red and yellow flames painted on its doors. Since he had taken over payments of the Corvette, it was a matter of transferring the ownership of the first car from my name to his. He took me to a dealership of some kind. I was made to wait in the car for a very long time while Dwight and another man worked out the transfer. I signed something that I didn't entirely understand. It didn't really seem to matter. After all, Dwight was paying for the car. What was strange was the subterfuge.

Some months later, Dwight was arrested for another very serious felony. Another felony followed that one, and he was looking at a jail sentence. Because I was still legally his wife, his car reverted to my care. My friends from church brought it home to my backyard, where it sat under a sheet of plastic. I finished buying it and later used it in an installation titled *Picnics*, which took flames as a recurring motif. I have always been fascinated by fire, from the time of watching the grass burn in our yard every spring in my childhood, through staring at fire dancing in the hearth of my home and the homes of friends, and then seeing the foot-long white flames darting from the ventilation holes in the gas kiln.

Fire is associated with warmth, danger, excitement, and purification. With suffering, too. It is a certainty that, during my short marriage and its long aftermath, I went through fire.

Of course, the flames on the Ford coupe's doors coincided with that imagery, and I wanted to include the car in my installation. I had already made a number of small ceramic tableaux set on little plots of ceramic grass. A few of these "picnics," which I sometimes think of as nice headstones, had flames in them. Artist friends I had met while I was teaching at UBC helped me enormously. Gloria Massé and Wendy Hamlin worked tenaciously with me to peel off the protective plastic sheeting that had more or less baked on the car while it sat in my yard. That was a formidable job. John Watts cleaned the undercarriage so that it wouldn't soil the floors of the Vancouver Art Gallery. I filled the interior of the car with ceramic watermelons—remembering those gorgeous, juicy watermelons in the summer fields of Hochfeld—and parked it on AstroTurf. That vintage car with its distinctive flames was used as evidence in Dwight's trial for rape, and in a sense helped to put him in prison for a long, long time. In the gallery, I set a ceramic sculpture beside it: a mantel clock with a big black bird sitting on top.

AFTER DWIGHT'S TRIAL and conviction, he was sentenced to serve a lot of time in jail. At first, he was in solitary confinement for his own protection. Although we had been separated for a couple of years, although he had been untrue to me, and although, too, he had committed this crime long after I asked him to leave, I believed it was my duty as his wife to find help for him when he was in trouble. That was the promise I had made, never imagining how bad things would get. I exerted a lot of effort to get Dwight out of the penitentiary into a rehabilitation program for sex offenders, which had recently been established in Matsqui prison. I wrote to the Solicitor General of British Columbia and to someone of the same consequence in Ottawa. After a few months, my efforts got him transferred out of solitary and into that more hopeful place, with lots of help and support from staff.

Every Saturday, I drove to Matsqui, which is near Abbotsford, was (minimally) checked out for contraband, and met Dwight near the coffee bar. He had a cup of coffee. I had coffee and a chocolate bar. The visiting room was like any large lounge with comfortable sofas and chairs. You could step outside into a fenced area if you wished. Women and children came to see their kin or their friends in an unstructured way. At some point, Dwight asked me to wear clothes that were more like those the other women visitors wore. I looked at them walking by in their jeans and boring tops. I didn't say anything in response. He could probably see I wasn't interested in looking like anyone else.

We discussed the past, we pulled apart many delusions, we did not fight. We went over the strange fact of his not working while we were together because he thought I made money so easily. Another truth that surfaced was that when he wasn't in jail, Dwight said, he felt like he was on a holiday and treated it as such—no working, lots of good times. The daily grind of real life was, for him, in jail. While he was living with me, he had several times tried to persuade me to rent out my basement suite to make some money. He knew just the right person, a woman friend of his—the hooker he'd brought to our home on Christmas Day. I resisted that idea. At the same time, I was thinking that he should be earning money in an honest way, something he had never done for any steady length of time.

In our zigzag way, I brought forward an idea that I had thought about a good deal. Since Dwight was my husband, I must continue to care for him but I didn't want him home with me ever again. Through the rehab program he was in, it might be possible that he could change into a different person. Still, I doubted this would be so. During one of our weekly visits, I took my courage into my hands and told him that when he had served his sentence, he should live on his own away from the city for a few years. He had previously let me know that he preferred small towns or suburbs to big city life. Since he had never lived alone, I thought he should learn how to do that and not rely on anyone else. If he could manage that, he could come back to my house. The last sentence was extremely difficult to say, but essential.

Dwight's face fell as I delivered my speech. He argued a bit, but I stuck to my proposition. I don't remember how we finished this session, but there were no blows and no tears. The following Saturday, I had an exhibition opening to attend at the Vancouver Art Gallery. I was showing *Picnics*. I told Dwight that I would have to miss our regular visit that day, but as it turned out I decided to skip what was to be a fantastic dinner following the opening reception, and went to see my husband after all. When I arrived at the prison, no one knew where Dwight was. I wasn't surprised by that, but I was astonished at how long it took to find him. Apparently he had been making hay with one of the nurses, something I worked out later. He wasn't very pleased to see me.

Around this time, Dwight asked me not to hug him during my visits. He also asked me to bring our wedding photos to him, so that he could show them around. Good-naturedly, I did. There was only one set of photos, a gift from old friends. As soon as Dwight had them in hand, he told me he was in love with a nurse in the rehab program. I was shocked and upset and asked for the photos back. He refused to return them. I knew what was in store. When Dwight had first come to my house after being released from jail, I was already in possession of his personal effects. There was a sizable box of photos from his past, including pictures of his first wedding. I have come to believe that he loved his first wife as much as he was capable of loving a person. We looked through the pre-wedding and wedding photos together and then, to my horror, he put the box into the fire in the fireplace. I thought he was being callous. He intended to show me he was through with that woman.

The photos were possibly the best part of my marriage. I looked just fine in the long white dress that Elizabeth had made for me, with my wedding pearls around my neck. Dwight looked unusually handsome in a white silk crepe shirt and dark trousers. My friends, despite their misgivings, had made a wonderful wedding cake. Dwight and I came into the church together, our guests following us hand in hand. Tom sang. It was a lovely wedding, blessed by my church. For all those reasons—and also because I have a reverence for history—I didn't want our wedding photos thrown into a fire. I wanted them back. Dwight told me not to be selfish and held them away from me. I should have shouted for help.

After that, there were no more hugs and kisses. We discussed his girlfriend and his second forthcoming trial. A nurse was always present during my visits. I remember saying, "When will we divorce?" Now it was Dwight who was shocked and upset. How could I think of such a thing? I replied that he was the one with the girlfriend—why wouldn't I be thinking about a divorce? Dwight's girlfriend had lost her job because the rules of employment were that staff did not become romantically involved with prisoners. To see each other, he would have to be sent back to the penitentiary. He requested the transfer. This move would allow his girlfriend to visit, not often, but regularly.

During this time, Dwight asked me not to visit him. Truthfully, I was relieved. We exchanged letters now and then, and a good while after his transfer, he asked me to send him some money. He wrote that he was going to make some craft items to sell. I was not pleased. I conferred with Glenn, who was pretty charged up hearing about the request. He had had a call from Dwight, asking him to get hold of some marijuana for Dwight to sell in prison. The cash I supplied was to buy marijuana, not craft supplies. I wrote a letter to Dwight spelling things out. The authorities must have seen it. Dwight was furious with me. I had betrayed him. He demanded a divorce. The game of checkers was almost over.

I requested help from UBC law students to draw up the divorce papers pro bono. The legal proceedings went on and on. Finally, in 1979, five years after I had married Dwight, I entered the provincial courthouse one day and was granted a divorce. Afterwards, I walked outside and down the block. As I passed the Toronto-Dominion Bank building, I looked up and saw two of my ceramic sculptures, visible through a window: a pyramid of apples and one of grapefruit. Seeing those sculptures felt like a big, bright affirmation of who I was. There is a sinking feeling, going through a divorce, acknowledging failure. But there was also a feeling of immense relief. In fact, I was glad it was over—and I've been glad ever since.

THAT QUIET MOMENT of celebration marked the end of my marriage but not the last time I saw Dwight. After serving enough time, he graduated to a less stringent penal institution where he had the opportunity to go on work assignments under some kind of supervision. One day, he knocked on my front door. He was just there to say hello, he said. We talked for a bit, and then he said he "had to dance," jumped into a prison vehicle, and drove off. That kind of visit happened now and then. Eventually he married the nurse from rehab and, sometime after that, visited me again. He excitedly urged me to see what was in the car. We walked down the steps to the road. I looked through the window, and there was a wee baby. Dwight was a proud father. I probably said something like, "Wow—that's great." Again, he left in a hurry.

More years passed before I got a phone call from him. Would I like to join him in a business venture? I would supply the cash, and he would make glass lampshades. I started to laugh and couldn't stop. Dwight made a few disappointed sounds, but eventually he joined me in great uproarious laughter. We talked a bit. His wife? No longer his wife. "I guess I'm not cut out to be a husband," he said. I agreed.

Many years after that, I was walking from the kitchen to the dining room, carrying dinner to the table. The radio news was on, and a voice said the RCMP were looking for Dwight. They named him. I almost dropped the dinner. My friends heard the broadcast too, and schemed to save me. Salmon Harris offered to sleep on my couch to protect me—very touching. Tom talked to the RCMP officer in charge of the case. He told Tom that Dwight had broken a young woman's leg while she was trying to escape from his car. Another flashy car. He also said that Dwight wasn't interested in any of his former wives and that I had nothing to worry about. And then he said that he was going to try to ensure that Dwight would be incarcerated for good.

My panic ebbed and things settled down again—at least for me.

PAINTING,

AGAIN

FOR A GLORIOUS MONTH in the spring of 1977, I was in Venice with Tom and Elizabeth. One day we took a train to Padua, mostly to look at Giotto's frescoes in the Arena Chapel. I was stunned by them—completely stunned. What affected me most were the paintings on the vaulted ceiling that depicted the vast heavens and the heavenly bodies. Giotto's sun, moon, and golden eight-pointed stars are set in a firmament of deep, rich, saturated blues—peacock and lapis lazuli. As I looked up at the ceiling in the Arena Chapel, the urge to paint was reborn in me after a hiatus of eleven years—eleven very full years of performance and installation and ceramic and wood sculpture. During the same trip, the sun sparkling on the green water in Venice also called out to me. *Night Skies* and *Pieces of Water*, however, had to wait a couple of years while I painted my glowing garden.

Gardens have been very consciously with me all my life, from the cherry trees in Hochfeld to the wild gardens of Northern

My painting studio, in the bedroom of my Kitsilano house, 1978. The works-in-progress, *East Border in Four Parts*, were inspired by my garden in glorious bloom and are now in the collection of the National Gallery of Canada in Ottawa.

Ontario, to my mother's formally laid out front yard in Winnipeg, with its circle and triangles of plants and flowers and its orderly paths lined with white stones. My mother also managed to persuade our various landlords to let her have tiny garden plots when we lived in rented rooms and apartments in Vancouver and, of course, she created abundant and blooming gardens in the yards of our houses on 31st and 51st Avenues. In almost all of these gardens, I was involved only as a spectator. Gardening, like cooking, had long been my mother's domain. As her health declined, so did the state of our yard, but after her death and my move to Kitsilano, I found myself braving the earthworms in order to make things grow again. Gardening became an entrancing occupation, which lasts to this day.

In April 1977, as I headed off on that revelatory trip to Italy, I had said goodbye to my gestating garden. When I came back a month later, it was in fantastic bloom. I got out my little Instamatic camera and took a series of shots, working my way a few steps at a time along each flower bed. When I looked at the developed photos, I noticed that each image slightly overlapped the previous one and I liked that effect. Both visually and conceptually, I could see that they grappled with time and light and point of view. Based on the photos, I made a series of big oil paintings, each consisting of three, four, or five panels, each panel with images overlapping from the one before. Initially, I was scared because I didn't know how I was going to paint after all those years. I didn't want the images to be too realistic; I wanted them to be somewhat flat, but I also wanted to convey abundant form, light, and colour.

In one series, I was particularly interested in the quality of late-afternoon light, when you can see halos around bushes and the tulips are almost transparent and strangely flattened. The paint in my new work was certainly not going to be thickly applied like my earlier, expressionistic paintings, but thinner, and with a different approach to the surface. For the areas of seemingly plain colour, such as the lawn and the sidewalk—not plain at all to my eye, I laid on lots of soft hues as underpainting, but I was not happy with the brushstrokes. I started to bounce the loaded brush on the surface, *thwack, thwack, thwack,* then gently brushed the thinned colours together. The effect was painterly, but not brushy.

Pierre Théberge, a curator at the National Gallery of Canada (NGC), visited my studio when I was still working on *East Border in Four Parts,* and he bought it right away. Because he had only seen my ceramic sculpture and my performance work, he was very surprised I was painting. I had the feeling he thought painting was a superior form of expression to everything else I had been doing. To me, ceramic sculpture, altered found objects, installation, performance, photography, and painting are all of a oneness: each medium is, I believe, the best possible for the particular image or idea I want to convey. And a number of my installations combine quite different media and materials, each part integral to the whole and all coming together to create a theatrical or immersive effect. In fact, that same year the NGC purchased my work, I borrowed the panels back to include in a mixed-media installation at Artcore, a new commercial gallery in Vancouver. The installation featured a dresser, a bed of sand, and a crowd of ceramic cabbages hanging from the ceiling on one floor. On another floor were all the panels from the *Borders* series.

As with my sculptures, performances, and installations, the images for my paintings come unbidden. Eventually Giotto's ceiling in the Arena Chapel did express itself through my own eyes and hands. When I was walking my dog at night, I would look up at the sky while she took her sweet time sniffing out the landscape. At some point, a voice in my head said, "Paint the sky! Paint the night sky!"

As meaningful as the images are to me, I realize I see colour first. I see colours that work together in balance and colours that jar, colours that have a dynamic effect and colours that have a softening effect. The combination of colour and form has to be strong. If it looks tired, I take it out. In 1979, I began to paint the night sky over the city, with its various shades of deep, rich blue, its scattered or hazy clouds infused with colour, suggesting reflections from the city below, and its twinkling stars, which I depicted as flat, five-pointed stars, a popular-culture form everyone recognizes.

I showed *Night Skies* in Calgary, Lethbridge, and Toronto, and at the Fine Arts Gallery at the University of British Columbia. Some critics and viewers thought the stars didn't belong in what they considered to be purely abstract colour-field paintings. At UBC, people even complained about them in the comments book accompanying the exhibition, to the point that my old teacher and mentor Jim MacDonald wrote me a letter to assure me that the paintings were wonderful. Ironically, people who saw the *Night Skies* paintings often tell me that now they look at the sky more keenly, and with more enjoyment. In these small ways, art has the power to transform our understanding of the world.

I followed *Night Skies* with *Pieces of Water*, which called up memories of light reflecting off the canals of Venice but are based on views of Vancouver's English Bay, which I would observe while, again, walking my little dog, Lady. I had the idea that each painting would depict a big chunk of water, which I had cut out of the sea with a long, sharp knife. The compositions are tilted up, so that shimmering colour fills the canvas, with no visible shore or horizon line. After *Pieces of Water* came some twenty more series of large paintings, approximately one series a year, some of the series with as many as twenty or thirty canvases in them.

When I took up painting again, I was working in a room in my house. In the early 1980s, however, I commissioned a friend, the architect Rob Mackenzie, to design a real studio for me where my garage had been. This meant taking down—with some sadness and apprehension—my big gas kiln, although I maintained and used my small electric kiln for a few more years. But building the new studio signalled my renewed commitment to painting.

MY FRIENDS
HUYEN
AND PHONG

IN 1979, I WAS part of a church group that sponsored two Vietnamese refugees to make their homes in Canada. This was during the time when many ethnic Chinese were fleeing Vietnam after the country fell to the Communists. There were numerous meetings among our small group, and many meetings too at Immigration Canada, where my patience was sorely tested by long, long waiting times. Waiting is always hard for me. How much harder it must have been for those in refugee camps, in difficult limbo and discomfort for months and years before being admitted to our country. Eventually, two young men arrived, cousins Huyen and Phong Ha.

Phong, being younger, adapted more quickly and learned English more easily. He was soon enrolled full-time in a high school. Huyen—pronounced Win—tried, somewhat unsuccessfully, to learn English in night-school classes for immigrants. He was very impatient with the teaching process and didn't think

Huyen Ha (on the left) and Phong Ha, sponsored refugees from Vietnam, in my Kitsilano house, 1979. How young and vulnerable they look.

he was learning quickly enough. As a consequence, he would bus across town at any time of the day to bring me a list of words he wanted to learn. I was working on my series of paintings *Night Skies* at the time but would set my brushes aside and go over the list of words with him. Teaching, after all, was a job not unknown to me. I also set up regular lessons with Huyen, who then came twice a week to my place. He and Phong often visited on Saturdays, and we shared dinners of crab or shrimp that they brought with them and prepared. I read to them and then asked them questions about the reading. Friends at UBC, Louise Fairley and Hani Henein, also dedicated a few nights a week to helping with both friendship and teaching. Other people in the group, including Elizabeth, picked up the challenge of entertaining our protégés on Saturday nights. We were instructing Huyen and Phong not only in English but also in cultural habits and mores. An evening spent with them was deeply rewarding but also very tiring.

Huyen's unannounced visits to my studio were taxing too, but I never turned him away. I had made a commitment. Early on he enrolled in an electronics course at a technical school, hoping to pursue work related to what he had done in Vietnam. He could partly understand Canada's quite different electrical regulations and methods if there were diagrams in the textbooks. However, he had to guess a lot at what was spoken in class and written in English. A number of times, he brought his books to my house, and I read the instructional material and tried to explain it. It was a strain on my brain, but Huyen seemed to be doing well in his studies. He graduated from the program with good marks and a fine recommendation. Still, he could not find work in his field. His limited English seemed to prevent him from securing a job. He then took a course in commercial cleaning and was having trouble understanding that too, so there I was one day demonstrating the finer techniques of window washing to him. I was myself fairly unacquainted with window washing, and it was an education for me, also.

My next foray into the business world found me driving Huyen to an interview and sitting in on it with him. I tried to explain to the prospective employer the basic language problems and also the training Huyen had taken. He was hired, but the job was moving boxes in a warehouse. He stuck it out until, with the help of his electronics teacher, he found another job installing alarm systems. But the new boss was bilking Huyen out of his lawful holidays. After that, there was an effort at making commercial awnings for a company that eventually was bankrupted, and other attempts to get ahead, including earning a licence to install and service gas fireplaces. During this difficult time, Huyen's marriage to his immigrant Chinese wife ended abruptly. Once she had earned her accountancy degree, she declared her need to live alone, which broke his heart. His sorrow took a toll on his mental health, and could be measured by the amount of liquor he put away.

Eventually Huyen was assisted by his younger brother, Jim, who had also arrived in Canada and who learned English very quickly. The brothers partnered in a small furnace business, which continues to this day. Huyen is not rich, but he is doing okay. Phong is doing better than okay: he is the head of a successful company that provides payroll services for businesses throughout North America. He is very busy and, with his loving wife and comfortable home, very happy.

I am still helping Huyen with his English: recently we've been reading Wayson Choy's memoir together. He comes to our house on Sundays and sweeps up the leaves in the courtyard. He brings fresh fruit and baby carrots and a chicken for roasting. His fingerprints are, metaphorically, all over our place—the studio, the garden, the house, the lighting inside and out. Out of pure kindness, he trims the small box hedges in the back garden, and the holly bush at the front door. He buys us big and ever bigger TV sets, which we have to refuse since we don't have the space to accommodate them. Over the years, he has repaid us in too many ways to count. He and Phong have become part of our home life, and Jim, too.

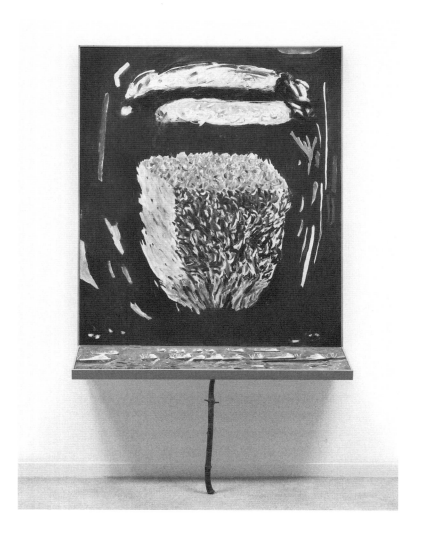

There Are 21 Ships and 3 Warships in English Bay, from my *Hedge and Clouds* series, 1990. I started these hinged paintings during a period when I walked along the water near my house every day and counted the freighters, barges, and warships at anchor.

HEDGE AND
CLOUDS AND
DEVELOPMENT
OF THE PLOT

I CONTINUED TO PAINT with great energy throughout the 1980s. Critics again observed that my subjects combined the real and the surreal, the everyday and the extraordinary. Wooden kitchen chairs with fish and maple leaves; big, soft chairs with men's suits and small bushes; grids of garden stakes adorned with bouquets; more grids of little spruce trees in pots with soup bones hovering over them. (This was a formal arrangement I also made into a three-dimensional mixed-media installation, with two-dimensional shadows painted across the floor and wall.) Venice hotel sinks with mirrors, postcards, and pink dresses; flowering trees and pillars of fire; tables set with bowls, fruit, flowers, birds, and carving knives—and casting long shadows; phases of the moon; apples, whole and in pieces; more night skies with moons and stars, the heavenly bodies cut out of aluminum or copper and affixed to the canvas.

Although I'd given up live performance and although, too, I'd taken apart my big kiln, performance and sculpture continued to influence my painting. In 1990, I brought an element of the third dimension, along with a note of political commentary, into my *Hedge and Clouds* series. Each work is composed of a large oil painting on canvas depicting, yes, oblong clouds hovering over a section of neatly trimmed hedge. Each work also has a narrow horizontal panel, which I attached to the bottom of the larger painting with hinges. On these narrow panels I painted ships I'd seen moored in English Bay. I thought of them as a kind of diary, because when I was still living in Kitsilano, I would walk every day along the water with my small dog, Lady, and count the freighters, barges, and warships I saw. Later, I incorporated the count into both the imagery and the titles of the individual paintings; for instance, *There Are 11 Ships and a Barge in English Bay* and *There Are 7 Ships and 2 Warships in English Bay*. As a pacifist, I found the presence of the warships very disturbing.

I propped the narrow hinged panels up with sticks I had made from the pruned branches of a wild cherry tree in my yard, creating "shelves" and nudging my paintings into the realm of sculpture. I was also looking at the painted hedges as sculptural, and as a curious play on the natural and the artificial. Unlike all my other paintings, these hybrid works were not well received at the time. I still have high hopes for them.

I first saw the different elements for the series of paintings I call *Development of the Plot* as a performance piece, with a beginning, a middle, and an end—a crescendo and a diminuendo—in the late 1960s. As I had originally envisioned the performance, a row of people would stand on one side of the room and another row of people would stand opposite them. They would all hold hypodermic needles upright in their hands, and they would advance on each other and then retreat, advance and retreat again, in a warlike way. However, I could never work out what they would do after that.

In *Drill*, the performance piece I created for the UBC Fine Arts Gallery in 1970 and later recreated in Calgary, the players held Popsicles in front of them instead of hypodermic needles, and had bunches of plastic flowers in their back pockets. Much more poetic, I thought.

Eighteen years later, I finally realized the imagery as a mural commission for Cineplex Odeon in North Vancouver and later as an extended, independent series of paintings. In *Development of the Plot*, the Popsicles became light bulbs. I used the recurring image of disembodied arms, hands raised and clasping golden light bulbs. I painted these images surrounded by theatrical motifs, such as stage sets, ropes, and props, incorporating the suggestion of a performance. I also added images of ziggurats and a lone man in a trench coat, one hand in his pocket and the other holding a book. Their positions shift, the man walking downstage towards us, the ziggurats floating up and back. Dogs and chairs make their way into these works, too.

Some of the elements in *Development of the Plot* came to me as I was sitting in a hospital emergency department, waiting with great anxiety while my dear friend Elizabeth was being examined for severe, unexplained pain. (The source of the pain was eventually diagnosed as the balling of scar tissue following earlier surgery. Excruciating, but not life threatening.) I quickly sketched out my ideas on paper—the paper from the bed of the examining room—and later developed them into a submission for a big mural project in Toronto. I didn't win that commission, but I thought the ideas were too good to abandon. In fact, the ideas completely absorbed me. Eventually, I created four suites of nine paintings each.

There was no dearth of public art commissions at that time. In the late 1980s, the architect Arthur Erickson had invited me to make a mural for a curving interior wall of a new building he was designing: the chancery of the Canadian Embassy in Washington, DC. I painted a big seven-panel work for it, a kind of diary of sequential and overlapping images of a bed of tulips in springtime, budding, blooming, fading, and drooping. At much the same time as *Development of the Plot*, I was also awarded a commission for a sculpture at Canada Place, on the Vancouver harbourfront. What I originally envisioned was poodles leaping through flaming hoops, imagery I'd previously explored in a series of paintings titled *Support Systems*. However, that idea was impractical as sculpture, and I ended up making two lions in cut aluminum, leaping through lit rather than flaming hoops. Although I have never been entirely happy with it, *Salute to the Lions of Vancouver* is a reference to the highly visible twin peaks on the North Shore Mountains.

I firmly believe that no matter what form it takes or material it employs, art enlarges possibilities. It creates new experiences and makes more keenly felt moments—glorious moments.

MY HOUSE—
AND BOB'S

IN THE MID-1980S, I resolved to build a new house of my own design. Sadly and coincidentally, my brother Gordon was sick with cancer at this time. For years, I had seen little of him or Jack or their wives and children—we had all been leading busy and separate lives—but Gordon's illness brought us closer together. Happily, I was invited to celebrate the anniversary of Edith, Gordon's first wife, and Harry, Edith's second husband. These two had been married for a long time, and Harry had helped raise Gordon's children.

The anniversary dinner was served at a big L-shaped table in a noisy restaurant. I sat at one end of the table with my niece Susan and her husband, David. We had a very good time, entertaining each other with stories. There was much laughter. I told them I had bought a property in East Vancouver, in what was then (but is no longer) an unfashionable neighbourhood. I explained that I was going to sell my house in Kitsilano and build a house that was

Holding my little dog Lady and waving brightly coloured dusters, I am leading a procession of friends through the front door of my half-built house, summer 1988. I was dedicating the house to be a place of welcome and joy.

suitable for my work, with a big studio and lots of storage space. This house would also accommodate my old age.

My nephew Bob was sitting at the other end of the table with his mother and Harry. I didn't know he could hear me over that distance and all the lively conversation and clatter in between. But when I finished my little exposition about planning a home and studio to my own specifications, Bob yelled, "Can I build your house?" I had no idea he was a builder, having been out of touch with him for so long. What could I say? Hesitation seemed inappropriate. I heard myself shout, "Yes!"

I never for a moment regretted the decision. He and his business partner, Garry Nicolychuk, did a fantastic job. Bob had built his own house in Burnaby, and he had also worked for many years taking houses apart, moving them to new locations and rebuilding them. He had spent a lot of time at the library too, researching old building methods. When my house was under construction, neighbours would walk by and say, "We haven't seen a house being built like this for fifty years or more." They were talking about the thick walls, substantial foundations, solid materials, beautiful framing and carpentry, and European-style stucco façade (which friends say resembles a French manor house). Bob asked me at every turn what I wanted: how wide the window frames should be, what kind and what size of baseboards there should be, how the grape arbour at the back of the house should be constructed. My aesthetic was pretty consistent: plain and simple in style but generous in size and materials.

I had taken a great deal of care and time drawing up the plans. I wanted things exactly right for me. I measured my furniture to see how much space it would take up. The social part of the main floor consists of a great room—living room, dining room, kitchen—with a row of windows at the front that look out onto our sloping front yard and tree-lined street, and a row of taller windows and French doors at the back that look out onto the grape arbour, courtyard garden, and studio. Tucked away from the great room, at the east end of the house, are a laundry room, bathroom, and small bedroom. Before Elizabeth moved in and I had a second bedroom and bathroom built upstairs, the top floor was a big, open, over-height storage space for my art. It is still an over-height storage space for my art, only not quite so big.

I fought with City Hall over building my studio in the backyard. After great effort, including letters to each council member, several meetings, and much worrying, I was able to get on with my project. I was told, "Don't make too much noise." I said, "I paint." Did I roll my eyes? Quietly?

An engineer friend, Heinz Klassen, also consulted with me about my plans. He offered to translate them into architectural drawings with specifications for the builders and also for City Hall approval. This was a great gift. By the end of March 1988, the plans were complete. The old house that had stood on the big property came down. It was a ramshackle old farmhouse with an unpaved basement floor that was more mud than dirt. Water kept spouting in, and we kept pumping it out. I was relieved that the place was in such bad condition because I don't like the idea of tearing down a livable house. Before it was demolished, I invited friends and neighbours to come in and take what they wanted. They didn't take a thing. Nothing was worth salvaging.

In the spring, Bob and Garry brought in big machines, and from then until the end of the following January, they worked like mad. A big hole was dug, strong foundations were built, a concrete floor was laid. I christened the foundations with coffee. Because I was working on two large public art commissions and a private one, along with the refurbishing and selling of my little house in Kitsilano, I was not always on the building site. When I came, I brought coffee and goodies and we all sat on the grass and, after it was built, on the doorstep. Elizabeth often came along too, and our two dogs sniffed things out.

There were many stages in the construction of the house, and I took pleasure in all of them. I remember when the wall frames first went up—all that fresh, bright wood, frames within frames, like a gorgeous, glowing, complex sculpture. This was the first time I had been able to closely examine a house under construction, and I revelled in the materials and the ways they were organized. My brothers were also interested, and they and Jack's wife, Vera, came to look one afternoon, before we all went on to dinner at a nearby restaurant. Jack appraised the building with his exacting eye for detail and had no criticisms of what he saw. Gordon surveyed the structure with his engineering mind and was proud of his son, Bob.

That summer, when the exterior walls of the first floor were done and you could walk from room to imaginary room—no interior walls, but each space beautifully laid out—it was time for a celebration. I invited ten friends and brought a lot of baking with me. We waited on the sidewalk for everyone to assemble. At that time, no one had ever entered through the front door. We had some decorative feather dusters on sticks. I taught everyone a Spanish dance step I had purloined, and we hopped and shuffled in, one at a time, waving our brightly coloured dusters. Once inside, I made a little speech about my intention that the house should be a place of comfort to all who visited—and a few other ambitious aspirations. We sang "Home! Sweet Home!" and a couple of other schlocky favourites. We probably disrupted the workers, but they didn't seem to mind. After our refreshments, we climbed the ladder to the unfinished top floor. We inhaled the rarefied air up there, checked out the view of the mountains, looked over the rooftops and treetops of the surrounding neighbourhood. It may have been small stuff to many, but the sense of home and belonging we were celebrating was hugely gratifying to me.

I had to sell the house in Kitsilano well before I could move into the new one, and for four months I lived with Tom and

Elizabeth who were then sharing a house close by, on Prince Albert Street. At that time, I could walk over to the building site, sweep the floor, and do a little painting, mostly of the window frames. The kitchen cupboards and the floors were out of my league. The floors in the living room and kitchen were cut out of maple plywood and spray-painted in the studio, glossy grey and white squares to be laid down in a checkerboard pattern. Garry did the spraying, and Bob did the sanding in between coats of paint. It was a lot of work. I wondered if I was crazy demanding painted checkerboard floors—not linoleum tiles or painted concrete but painted wood, which is so much warmer. As much trouble and labour as my new floors caused Bob and Garry, they were wonderfully gracious about it and did a superb job.

There was a time when the house was filled with plumbers and electricians. (I was delighted to be able to have as many electrical outlets as I had ever wished for.) Then another team of workers arrived to put on the exterior stucco. I showed them what I wanted: a flat, plain surface painted a soft Provençal yellow. The only decoration was a tile border on the exterior walls of the house and the studio, which required a good bit of work. I had started making the tiles in my studio in Kitsilano but had taken a break from that job to put in my new garden. Elizabeth took over the tile making, mixing the materials and putting them into moulds. She also helped me with planting seedlings. The plasterers then started on the inside of the house, making white walls, working every day of the week. Speed was important because I was insisting on moving in by the end of January, my birthday.

The last few days were very grim for Bob and Garry, as they installed the wooden checkerboard floor in the great room. The beautifully painted tiles had to fit exactly and stay put after they were glued. The guys laid down half the floor with glue that did not dry immediately, and the tiles floated away from the spots they were set on. Quickly, with no time for anger or frustration, they pulled up all the tiles and started over with a fast-setting glue. This time the tiles fit snugly, from side to side and end to end. When the floor was laid, Bob and Garry were so exhausted that they took the next few days off and let me put on several coats of very hard varnish to protect the painted surface.

The day before I moved in, Elizabeth hung the curtains she had made for me. I was in and out, marvelling at the shiny grey-and-white checkerboard floors, the white walls, and the tall windows, front and back and at the corners.

On moving day, my friends Wendy Hamlin and Rob Mackenzie helped carry boxes into the house, always delivering them to the right rooms. I remember sorting tableware in the kitchen and Wendy throwing out things she didn't think I needed, which I, of course, retrieved. Elizabeth was there in the thick of it, and Tom and his sister brought lunch. Tom put a gorgeous carpet on the top of a table and laid out a lovely meal. I was very happy and very tired and came down with a heavy cold. I celebrated my birthday alone, resting in my new house and taking short walks in my new neighbourhood.

When I was well again, I threw a small housewarming party for family and a few close friends. My nieces Carol and Susan gave me what I wanted: posts for the fences to be put up later. Tom brought a few funny signs and put them up here and there. They read "Bob Hates This and Garry Does Too." One of the sources of their displeasure was my insistence on using long, dark nails to hold up the curtain rods. (The long, dark nails are still there, still holding up the curtain rods.) We all laughed.

After I moved in, there were daily revelations of the miracle of my new home. I looked again and again at the shiny grey-and-white floors, and thought over and over how lucky I was. In my prayers, I thanked God for the house. And—perhaps perfidiously selfish and self-centred—I asked to be able to keep it. Thirty years later, I am still here.

An installation shot of *Traces* at the Equinox
Gallery, 1998. As I worked on the dresses, a
story about them took form in my mind.

TRACES
(WITH PAPER
AND PASTE)

AFTER I HAD DEVOTED some eighteen years straight to painting, a new idea dropped into my head. What I saw, fully formed, was a sculpture of a woman's dress, almost life-size, with two cuts in the skirt bottom, raised up a little to make a shelf. On the shelf, there would be an orange or some other small object. Given the size of the dress I envisioned—and the image pressed on my mind for a couple of years before I resolved how to realize it—I could see that clay would be too heavy for it, too impractical. And it would undoubtedly break during firing—that is, if I could find somewhere to fire it since I had dismantled my big gas kiln.

I thought of papier mâché, a lowly medium most often associated with children's craft projects, not with fine arts, not with professional artists. My choice was not an Arte Povera political statement, however; it was purely practical. I had learned how to use papier mâché when I was a schoolteacher. I knew the basics: newspaper strips covered in wallpaper paste or a cooked mixture of flour and water, the strips modelled around a form of some sort. Light, malleable when wet, strong when dry, paintable, portable— and no need for a potentially disastrous kiln firing. It was perfect. I soaked the newspaper strips in liquid cellulose and valued the stories and images that would appear in the pages of the papers and disappear into my sculptures. They folded all kinds of histories into the work. The painted and glazed surface of the hardened papier mâché suggests skin, the subtle shadows and hills and valleys of the forms suggest flesh—just as glazed ceramic had done previously.

Not one of the six dresses I made has an orange on the shelf of the skirt. One, which the Vancouver Art Gallery acquired, has insects in a box, which is tilted on its shelf. Another has a row of singing birds. Others have a photo of a boy, a woman's shoe, toiletry items, and four lit candles with two additional candles on the shoulder blades. This last dress is in the collection of the National Gallery of Canada.

When I started making the papier mâché sculptures, I didn't have anything to stand them on. I hung a rope from the ceiling and attached a coat hanger to it and worked from there. It was far from ideal as it kept twirling. My friend and fellow artist John Watts came over and said, "No, no, that will never do." As has happened so often, he figured out what I would need and made me a secure support from an old I.V. stand. It worked beautifully.

As I developed the dresses, the plan for an installation emerged—and so did a story. It seemed to me that someone had travelled across the country, from one end to the other, in search of the dresses, which had been left behind in closets. Some of the owners had died; others had moved away. Each dress was empty of a body but retained a bit of space inside, and slightly collapsed contours outside, to indicate the wearer's presence: traces of women's lives. In the installation, which I called *Traces*, the dresses would stand in a row, on plinths in the middle of the gallery, with images and objects on three walls around them. On one tall wall, there would be three paintings of two parts each: crossed ankles with red sandals below; four midriffs with two belts below; and two pairs of shoulder blades with two enormous corsages above. Against another wall, there would be a high bench about seven feet long (built by my nephew Bob) with a number of papier mâché articles on it, including a gardenia corsage in a box, a high-heeled shoe, and a folded nightdress. And on the third wall, floor to ceiling, was to be an immense grid of identical black-and-white photographs, silkscreened on vellum, of a woman's crossed ankles and feet clad in well-worn slip-on shoes. The photos are poster-size and hang like shingles, fastened at the top and loose at the bottom, each one slightly overlapping the photo below. If you walk briskly past them, they lift slightly in the breeze, suggesting the movement of a skirt, a whole crowd of skirts.

I thought I would put a kitchen chair on the floor near the entrance to the gallery. And then something new came to me: a pair of women's shoes standing on the floor next to the chair. Then I caught myself, a voice in my head saying, "Save it, fool! You have enough stuff in the room!" I showed *Traces* at the Equinox Gallery, and again in my big retrospective exhibition at the Vancouver Art Gallery. It then travelled to Regina, Halifax, Oshawa, Fredericton, and the National Gallery of Canada in Ottawa. *Traces* struck people as a meditation on femininity, a subject I may have touched on in my early performances but had never fully explored before. Critics also saw loss, melancholy, and death in it—as they did in so many of my works. Inevitable, I suppose.

Sitting in the sunshine at the University of British
Columbia with, left to right, Gloria Massé, John
Watts, and Wendy Hamlin. They were among a
group of my students who became lasting friends
and mutually supportive colleagues.

MY
COMMUNITY
(FRIENDS,
DEALERS,
COLLECTORS)

WHEN I WAS YOUNG, through my teens and twenties, my social life revolved around my church. It offered friendship and companionship, shared values, and many happy activities. In the late 1960s, as I became increasingly committed to making art, my close friends were mostly outside the church—and inside the art world. I established close bonds with my teachers, mentors, and fellow artists; with the students and colleagues who collaborated with me on big projects; and as my career progressed, with writers, critics, collectors, and art dealers. Early on, Glenn Lewis, Michael Morris, Tom Graff, Glenn Allison, and Salmon Harris all became part of my new community. So did Elizabeth Klassen, a fellow public school teacher whom I first met while taking summer courses in Victoria and who was drawn into our circle of art-making and performance. The years that I shared a house with Tom and Elizabeth, in the early 1970s, were a time of creative ferment—a continuous flow of friends and coffee, and of taking pains to celebrate small and large occasions. There was much help given and received on all sides.

In the mid-1970s, when I taught part-time in the bachelor of fine arts program at the University of British Columbia, I developed lasting friendships with some of my students, including Barry Jones, Rob Mackenzie, Marjorie MacLean, Gloria Massé, John Watts, and Wendy Hamlin. Through long conversations with Gloria, John, and Wendy, many of them in a basement lunchroom on campus, we discovered that we had all had religious educations. And although they had each fallen away from their church, that shared background was the cement that first bonded us. The four of us met frequently for years, first every week, then every month, and now, some forty years later, when we can. John is still in Vancouver, but Gloria lives on Gambier Island off the Sunshine Coast, and Wendy, near Naramata in the Okanagan Valley. We have spent many long hours talking and critiquing each other's work, and, on two occasions, we have exhibited our art together.

Along with four other friends, Wendy and Gloria helped me immensely in the production of an enormous commission for the BC Central Credit Union in Vancouver. This work, which I titled *Beautiful British Columbia Multiple Purpose Thermal Blanket*, is essentially an immense "quilt" of fifty-six painted canvas panels, stuffed with insulation and stitched together. The individual panels include depictions of my neighbourhood, porches, sidewalks, fences, lawns, and flower gardens—especially flower gardens. I called the work a "sculpted painting." After completing it, I used the same ideas and format to create eight *Beautiful British Columbia Thermal Blankets* on a slightly smaller scale, eight feet square. Each was composed of nine painted squares with a broad green border, and in each of the nine squares, I painted similar flower and garden motifs, then added images of the friends in my life. Many of these were based on snapshots I had taken at tea parties, birthday parties, and Christmas dinners. All the happy events and ritual celebrations at which we enjoyed shared food and drink and took pleasure in each other's company.

In addition to my fellow artists, I count my dealers among my circle of friends. My connection with Avrom Isaacs, the director of the Isaacs Gallery in Toronto, took a few years and a little back-and-forth dance to complete. When I was showing my ceramic *Fruit Piles* in Vancouver in 1970, Av approached me about exhibiting work in his gallery and becoming my Toronto dealer. I said no, I preferred to handle the sale of my own work. We had a few more discussions in the ensuing years, but either he was interested and I wasn't, or vice versa. Finally in the early 1980s, when Av approached me once again, I was good and willing to work with him. Too many people had trailed through my house looking at paintings, sometimes buying them, sometimes not, following my exhibition of *Night Skies* at the UBC Fine Arts Gallery.

Of course, we had to come to some terms. The one that mattered most to Av was that my prices had to go up. My prices did go up. They doubled, to the great annoyance of Elizabeth Nichol, who was then the director of the Equinox Gallery. She had been buying my work outright and then reselling it to her clients, and she was worried that they wouldn't be willing to pay as much as collectors in Toronto. And perhaps that was so. For a number of years, I sold more paintings in Toronto than in Vancouver, yet Av used to say that I would die a pauper. I was very sorry when Av closed the Isaacs Gallery in the early 1990s to focus on the Innuit Gallery instead, but he and his wife, Donnalu Wigmore, remained my good friends. We visited each other and exchanged letters. Avrom Isaacs died in January 2016. I have yet to get over that loss.

Having given the Isaacs Gallery exclusive rights in Toronto, I felt I had to give the Equinox Gallery the same deal in Vancouver, and I continue to show with that gallery to this day. Elizabeth Nichol was a lovely person, friendly and kind. Her death in

2000 was also a blow, and a great loss to the art community. Andy Sylvester is now the owner of the Equinox Gallery, and I count him and the surviving Nichols as friends, too. Andy organized a spectacular survey of my work in 2015. One room in the gallery was wholly dedicated to my *Pieces of Water* series of paintings from 1981. This was the work that tipped me into full gallery representation.

Of all the people who have collected and still collect my work, I was closest to Ron Longstaffe. He not only acquired my work for himself but also bought and donated it to the Vancouver Art Gallery. A big man with a booming voice and considerable influence, he was responsible, too, for my receiving a number of awards and honours. It is very important to me to commemorate him here: he was a great friend and the only collector who continued to buy my work even after his house was full. He gave away what he could not show at home.

In 2002, Ron became very ill with cancer. He was soon hospitalized with a broken leg, the cancer having spread to his bones. Elizabeth and I visited him many times. At Ron's bedside, we often met one of his friends who bestowed on him small gifts in brown paper bags. Ron gave us a number of gifts too: a clock that rings the hours with birdsong, and a bell that hangs outside in our garden. I was impressed to discover that he had also donated a goodly sum of money to St. Paul's Hospital, where he died.

Ron died in the spring of 2003, less than a year from the beginning of his illness. Now, on windy days when the bell in the garden thrashes about, pealing loudly, I think of him.

BLESSINGS, OR THE MYSTERIOUS CHRONICLES OF A BROKEN ARM

ONE HOT JULY DAY in 1997, when I was in the middle of making my papier mâché dresses, I was walking to the market with Elizabeth and a neighbour. Elizabeth's dog, Emma, was trotting along with us. Suddenly the sidewalk reared up and hit me. Well, actually, as I turned to hear what our companion was saying, my foot caught on the crumbling edge of the sidewalk and I fell and broke my right arm—the arm with which I paint and draw and sculpt and write and, well, do everything. I broke two bones in my upper arm, near my shoulder. I was in ghastly pain, lying on the sidewalk. Everyone was shouting, "Don't move! Don't move!" Neighbours phoned for help and stood over me to create shade, protecting me from the vicious sun. I remember belting out "When Irish Eyes Are Smiling" to distract me from the pain.

An ambulance arrived, and I was given laughing gas and taken to the nearest hospital. A doctor attended to me and then sent me home, where my stomach reacted violently to the pain and the

Witnesses Protecting the Broken Arm from the Sun: Diana, Elizabeth, Judith, Rebecca. From the series *The Mysterious Chronicle of the Broken Arm,* 1997. Gouache on paper, 24.0 × 34.0 cm.

pain medication. For three weeks, I couldn't keep food down. And the trauma was not just physical. My mind was filled with fear and despair. The air around me was heavy and gloomy. From then on, I was convinced, I would keep falling and breaking my bones. This accident was certainly the beginning of the end for me. I cradled my arm as if it were a sick baby. I was afraid of people coming near me because I didn't want to be jostled. And I didn't want to go outside at all. I didn't trust my feet to carry me across the ground safely. Eventually, very eventually, Elizabeth talked me into going outside with her. I clung to her arm, desperately anxious. My mind was as sick as my arm, but it healed, just as my arm healed, stronger than ever.

After the accident, my friends rallied around me magnificently. John Watts arrived with a blue sling for me, and Sylvia Beech, from our church, came to the house to give me physiotherapy. She assigned me a couple of gentle exercises to do three times a day, and also rubbed my arm in all the right places. (Evidently her therapy worked: a doctor had told me I would never again be able to raise my arm above my shoulder, but Sylvia's ministrations and exercises enabled me to regain the full use of it.) Tom and his partner, Antony Porcino, brought cookies, and my niece Susan Falk spent what must have been a week's income on art magazines, sunflowers, soap, and other good things. Huyen Ha offered rides and a second-hand Lincoln Continental, and his wife washed my hair, taking pride in producing a wave. Ann Rosenberg arrived with asparagus and a potato salad, and a drawing of her new house on Pender Street. Elvira Wiebe drove me to the doctor; Jeremy Wilkins brought bags of cat food; Charmian Johnson, pottery and baklava. My nephew Bob and his wife, Iris, also brought goodies, and Bob helped me with stamps for my letters, while Iris shortened a slip so that I could wear it as a skirt in the broiling hot weather. It was so hot that Elizabeth was baking pies at night, using the peaches that had ripened on the espaliered trees behind my studio. And, of course, she did everything else at home: offered food to friends, ran all the errands, cooked and washed, and watered the large garden.

Occasionally, I would go into my studio and just finger *Dress with Singing Birds*, the papier mâché sculpture I had been working on before my accident. I couldn't push forward with it, though, because it required the use of both hands. For a long time, I lay on the sofa in misery, doing nothing, completely inert and depressed. One day, though, when Eva Winkler, the woman who cleaned our house, was vacuuming the rug at the front door, my mind said, "Eva, with blessings." I sat up and began to use my left hand to draw all my recent blessings—all my dear friends who brought me cheer and comfort. I began with Elizabeth in the kitchen in her shorts, a pie in each outstretched hand, and called it *Elizabeth, Stealing the Night*.

When I was able to eat normally again, most of the gloom disappeared. There was a beautiful bouquet of flowers on the table, brought home from the farmers' market. I was moved to paint it, and although I had never used gouache before, it seemed like it would be the right medium. I phoned a friend, Miranda Mallinson, who brought me the paint and laid it out for me on a wheeled table. John brought an easel. I had already been using my left hand to write letters (badly) and make ink drawings in my sketchbook (strangely); now, I could make the drawings of my accident and subsequent blessings in colour.

It was a joy to mix the gouache and make pictures, combining the real, the metaphysical, and the spiritual. There's always a heavenly presence in these works, an angel hovering above or flying past. I called the series *The Mysterious Chronicles of a Broken Arm*. Odd as they are, these gouaches on paper are among my favourite paintings. They broke the nasty spell of misery and inactivity. After a while, I returned to the studio and resumed soaking strips of paper in paste. I was making art again.

MY
EXHIBITIONS,
RETRO-
SPECTIVELY

MAKING ART IS, for me, a necessity. Exhibiting art, though not so much a necessity, feels like a consolidation of its purpose, as if the audience viewing it were also completing the cycle of its existence. Since 1965, I have been honoured with more than fifty-five solo shows, in public and commercial galleries, in Vancouver, across Canada, and beyond. I've also been blessed with some major retrospective exhibitions—providing occasions for review and reminiscence.

My first big retrospective was in 1985 at the Vancouver Art Gallery. It was simply titled *Gathie Falk Retrospective* and covered some twenty years of my career, from my early expressionistic oil paintings of the 1960s through my installation and ceramic sculptures of the 1970s, and on to my somewhat surrealistic paintings of the mid-1980s. (Cabbages suspended over green velvet chairs, fish tied to wooden kitchen chairs, light bulbs hanging above rows of flowering bushes.) Jo-Anne Birnie Danzker,

Installation view of *Gathie Falk Retrospective*,
exhibition at the Vancouver Art Gallery, 1985.

who had been a curator at the VAG when the project was initiated but was its director when the show opened, interviewed me at length about my early life and the launch of my art career. Using her transcribed interviews, I wrote a long personal essay for the exhibition catalogue, a kind of artist's statement in the form of autobiography. (Those interviews and that essay have been a rich resource for this memoir too.) My old friend and colleague Tom Graff contributed notes and remembrances about my performance art to the catalogue, and the curator Scott Watson wrote an essay titled "Gathie Falk's Sources and Rituals." I can't pretend I liked Scott's essay. He drew likenesses between my art and my church that I thought were untrue to my intentions. Still, the show looked wonderful. I was proud of it. A condensed version of it, *Gathie Falk: Painting Retrospective*, appeared at the Art Gallery of Greater Victoria that same year and then toured.

In 1999, the VAG offered me a second retrospective exhibition, which was scheduled to open in February 2000 with a major publication accompanying it. This was a happy surprise to me: I had very low expectations of the new millennium. The VAG's Bruce Grenville was to curate the show, and Robin Laurence, an ace writer and art critic, was to provide the long critical biography that ran through the book. Others—Bruce, Ian Thom, Mayo Graham, and Sarah Milroy—would contribute short essays about individual artworks. Many of my paintings, sculptures, and installations were to be photographed or re-photographed for the book, a number of the photos to be taken by the talented Teresa Healy. For many months leading up to the show, I worked closely with Bruce and Robin, going over the works to be included and talking at length—again—about my life and art. I was excited about the prospect of a second and much larger retrospective and completely absorbed in its creation.

In the middle of these preparations, in September 1999, seemingly out of the blue I received a phone call from Rimouski,

Quebec. Where? Apparently, a couple of years earlier, I had agreed to have a show in this small city on the St. Lawrence River, in the Musée régional de Rimouski. What? I had entirely forgotten about it. That show was to open before Christmas, and I had to scramble to put something together for it. The VAG refused to lend anything, seeing that it needed my stuff for its retrospective. I assembled a show from works I owned and what Rimouski could borrow from public and private collections. We ended up with three of my eight-foot-by-eight-foot *Beautiful British Columbia Thermal Blankets*, a wall full of small light bulb paintings on wood (which I had made for the big local exhibition known as Artropolis), some *Venice Sinks with Postcards from Marco Polo*, a couple of paintings from my *Soft Couches* series. It amounted to a grab bag of a survey.

I flew to Rimouski for the installation and opening of *Gathie Falk: Souvenirs du quotidien*, and talked to students. As they spoke only French, and I, only English with a bit of garbled French remembered from grade school, there was no small talk. After the opening, I celebrated with the bilingual staff, who kindly spoke English to me. Later, lost in a shopping mall, I struggled to ask for directions in French. A woman, a stranger, answered me in perfect English. One can but wonder at such separate worlds with their tiny knots of understanding. In my mind, I blessed her.

The second VAG retrospective covered three decades of my career, from a restored and restaged version of *Home Environ-ment* to *Reclining Figure (after Henry Moore): Stella*, a papier mâché dress I had just completed. Hordes of people attended the opening, and there was interest from all the media—TV, print, and radio. People lined up around the block to get into the open-ing reception, and to get into the show for many weekends after that. Later it would also go on to tour across the country, where it made a particularly big splash at the National Gallery in Ottawa. After the big public reception, there was a smaller and more personal party at my house, the guests including Andy Sylvester; Av Isaacs; the publisher Scott McIntyre and his wife, Corky; Ron Longstaffe and his wife, Jacqueline; the Nichols; and lots of family and friends.

The happiness I felt at the success of my retrospective was short-lived, however. I'd seen my nephew Bob only briefly at the public opening. At the party at my house, I got a closer look at him. He was yellow. I wasn't sure what that meant, but I knew it was not good. We soon learned that Bob had rampant and incurable liver cancer. The first clue that something might be wrong had come the previous Christmas when Bob thought he had stomach flu because he couldn't keep food down. After his diagnosis, he cried on my shoulder, almost the only sign he made of his distress. Like my brothers, he was heroic in living each day well. He got up and dressed every morning, and though he might lie on the living room floor for short rests, he was never in bed. He drove to my house in Vancouver, where he enjoyed our talks and debates, as he had done even in childhood. Or he went to his sister's place in Langley, where he helped Susan and her husband, David Turner, put up a new barn. One Friday in November, Bob went to a chiropractor with Iris, his wife. Two days later, we were asked to come to Burnaby General Hospital to say our goodbyes. Bob was talking about work, as if in a dream. On Monday, he died. Very soon after, my art dealer Elizabeth Nichol died of Parkinson's disease, from which she had suffered for many years. The winter of 2000 was very bleak.

Earlier that fall I had travelled to Pense, Saskatchewan, with Andy Sylvester, who had commissioned a series of bronze sculptures from me to be sold through the Equinox Gallery. This was a new medium for me, and we were there, at the foundry owned by the widely acclaimed artist Joe Fafard, to supervise the patina application of the first edition of my bronze dresses. The foundry was a fascinating place. There was the pit for dipping the wax model in the slurry, the burnout oven for melting the wax from the ceramic mould, the furnace for heating the bronze ingots, and another pit where the molten bronze is poured into the mould. And the staff were warm and friendly, people one could very much like.

On a walk in the countryside near Pense, to while away the time as the foundry workers were hard at it, I looked at the autumnal fields in the late afternoon light: beautiful wide stretches of straw yellow, dull green, and grey under a pale blue sky. The colours and the landscape made me think of Agnes Martin's paintings. And, of course, although she made her career in the United States, she had been born in rural Saskatchewan. I would call the dress, in its edition of seven, *Agnes*. One of the castings, which was intended to be shown indoors, was finished in a lovely, rich blue. As soon as I saw it, I took some Kleenex and rubbed off the colour on the places I wanted highlighted. Another dress was to have a pale yellow patina, which turned out an awful muddy colour. I hated it, but the man in charge said they wouldn't or couldn't change it. Do what I might to rub it off, it remained a dreadful colour. I felt ill, physically and emotionally.

On the plane ride home with Andy, he and I talked about the yellow dress. He asked me whether I liked it. I told him exactly how I felt and then said they couldn't change it. He said, "Nonsense!" He would fix it. After that I no longer asked for a pale-yellow or dark-blue patina, but chose grey and black for the remaining bronzes, which all sold well. A black *Agnes* stands comfortably in my backyard, among various vines and leaves.

I had been uneasy going to Saskatchewan while Bob was so ill. Afterwards, however, I was glad because he was able to see one of my bronze dresses before he died. He came to my studio and met my blue *Agnes* with her tissued-off highlights. He was the best audience I could have asked for. And exactly the note of completion the work required.

PORTRAITS,
SHIRTING,
BASEBALL
CAPS

IN HOMAGE TO MY nephew Bob, I began a series of nine men's shirts sculpted in papier mâché. I had noticed that he, like many other men, habitually wore the same style and make of shirt. Bob and his brother-in-law and business partner, Garry Nikolychuk, wore short-sleeved shirts in plaids or checks. My art dealer Andy Sylvester wore expensive long-sleeved white shirts with a quietly spotted red tie. My friend Edward Kehler, on the few occasions in which he dressed up, wore a white shirt with a blue bow tie. Antony Porcino, the partner of my friend Tom Graff, wore coloured stripes; John Watts wore plain black; Elizabeth Nichol's husband, John, white, again with a blue bow tie. Jake Kerr, one of my loyal patrons, wore white shirts with fine blue stripes and a red dotted tie; my brother Jack wore light-coloured, fine-striped shirts with a diagonally striped tie. I realized that I was portraying these individuals through their characteristic and somehow symbolic garments, and called the series *Portraits*.

An installation shot from *paperworks*, my solo
exhibition at the Burnaby Art Gallery, 2014. The
papier mâché shirt in the foreground was made
as an homage to my nephew Bob Falk. Behind it
are some *Shirting* paintings on vellum.

The shirts are free-standing, like the dresses before them, slightly smaller than life size—and also a bit flatter, though on occasion they seemed to take on the shape of the person who would have worn them. For example, my brother Jack was over eighty at the time I made his shirt, and he had a slightly stooped back. I had no intention of portraying him in that posture and modelled the shirt upright. The shirt, however, had a will of its own and turned out with a slightly stooped back too.

For my exhibition of *Portraits*, I stood the shirts in a row facing the back of the room. The left wall was hung with large oil paintings of simple roses, each functioning as a kind of light, one for each shirt. On the opposite wall were black-and-white photos of the rose paintings, like shadows. It was a satisfying experience for me to give these shirts—these men—special attention in this way.

By 2002, I was making a series of paintings that I called *Shirting*. I had been so impressed by the patterns in men's shirts when I was working on *Portraits* that I went off on an excursion into acrylic painting on vellum. My technique was to lay the vellum over hand-drawn black lines and then paint thinned acrylic between these lines, so that they would be straight but still bear the mark of my hand. My first experience was a shock: when the vellum became wet it stretched and wrinkled, making little bumps in some places and little sinkholes in others where the paint pooled. I was dismayed: my plans for simple stripes, checks, and plaids on a flat ground were defeated. But then—*What! What! What!* When the paint and vellum dried, the effect was a marvellous cloth-like texture, almost like seersucker, with a strange glow, as if lit from behind. I loved the result.

I showed a large series of my *Shirting* paintings at the Equinox Gallery in 2002. Many of them were eight feet long, hung unframed on the wall like scrolls. At the top of each, I had folded the vellum over a thin strip of wood, secured it with bulldog clips, and suspended the work from a tack with a piece of kitchen string.

The paintings hung loose and sometimes ran out onto the floor. I liked the ordinariness of this presentation, but people had a hard time getting their minds around the work. I thought the patterns alone should have been enough. They became saleable only when they were cut down in size and framed. Another kind of ordinariness.

In 2003, following *Shirting*, I began making *Baseball Caps*. I was interested in the different colours, materials, logos, and fasteners—and what the caps said about the people who wore them. But mostly, I liked the way the close-fitting old-fashioned ones are made in segments like an orange. The size and shape of the peak are also important to my eyes. Many of my friends loaned me their baseball caps to work from. I sculpted individual baseball caps in papier mâché and also painted pictures of them in acrylic on paper. In showing the work, I mounted a grid of the cap paintings on a large "wallpaper" ground of tar paper that I had painted in a pattern of vines and leaves in dull browns and greens. Some of the other paintings were framed, and the sculpted caps were presented on plinths in the middle of the room.

I was delighted with the way the exhibition looked, but also saddened. One of the caps I borrowed and sculpted belonged to my good friend and patron Ron Longstaffe. As I was working on the show, he was diagnosed with the cancer that would kill him. His illness cast a shadow across an otherwise cheery undertaking.

MY FRIEND
ELIZABETH

ELIZABETH AND I might have been sisters, so akin are we in our tastes, beliefs, and experiences. We were born in the same year to Russian Mennonite parents and raised in Manitoba, our families struggling to make ends meet and eventually seeking a more fruitful life in British Columbia. Elizabeth, however, was born in Russia, her parents fleeing to Canada when she was a year old, on one of the last ships out before Stalin closed the borders. She did most of her growing up in Elie, a farming community about an hour's drive west of Winnipeg. Her father worked for very little money as a farm labourer before acquiring his own farm, through the help of his wife's family. Elizabeth remembers early years living in a rented house that had been converted from a granary, with unfinished wood siding on the outside and bare studs on the inside. Like me, she also remembers cold winters, with frost forming on the inside of the windows.

Elizabeth at our front door and, behind her,
a slice of the big garden she has cultivated.

Elizabeth's mother died when she was six and her younger sister was four. Her father remarried not a wicked stepmother but a lovely, clever, and resourceful person. Elizabeth's father wasn't a very good farmer, she says, but the family scraped along through the Depression when so many others were just scraping along too. In the 1940s, Elizabeth's family, which by then included an adopted son, picked up and moved west, her father having given up on growing grain. They struggled there too, on a small farm near Chilliwack, surviving the 1948 flood of the Fraser River. Their house was badly damaged, but with the flood relief the government provided, they repaired it and restarted their farm.

For a while, Elizabeth worked in a chicken hatchery, then moved with a friend to Vancouver—again, a place that seemed to promise glorious things. She cleaned houses as a day labourer and then found a full-time job in the kitchen of Vancouver General Hospital, saving enough money to go to Normal School. She taught for a number of years in a little schoolhouse in Kispiox, in Northern British Columbia, and, as I did, took summer courses towards a bachelor of education degree.

When I was attending summer school in Victoria, I shared a long attic room with three other young women teachers. During my second summer there, Elizabeth joined us. It was great fun—like living in a dormitory. We all sang, our voices ringing out in three-part harmony. Elizabeth and I went to a performance of Marcel Marceau, the famous French mime, and later we entertained our roommates with stories and imitations. The group of us spent our non-studying time singing, discussing challenging ideas at dinner, and heading off on adventures crammed into Sally's Volkswagen. Elizabeth and I both enjoyed classical music and good-looking clothes. We had the same religious background and foreground. And we both loved to laugh.

We were both avid readers too, and loved the same books and authors—Henry James, Jane Austen, the autobiographical writings of Canada's most famous woman artist, Emily Carr. Elizabeth will never live down her innocent remark about Carr: "Didn't she also paint?" As a child, on occasional trips with her family to Winnipeg and back to the farm, Elizabeth enjoyed a big rich pudding of new reading: the billboards lining the roads. I was luckier than she in having access to the Winnipeg Public Library and also to newspapers and magazines that Gordon salvaged for us. There was little to read in Elizabeth's family's house.

We have shared many living spaces—filled, of course, with books and art. Elizabeth loaned me the money for the down payment on my 51st Avenue house, and lived with me there during the two years it took her to complete her bachelor of education degree at the University of British Columbia. Later, Tom Graff and Elizabeth both rented suites in my Kitsilano house: Tom downstairs and Elizabeth up. We mostly gathered on the main floor where I lived. There, we ate and made merry and occasionally argued. We are all short and our friends started to call us The Little People.

Elizabeth took part in the performance pieces that we developed and organized in that house and, of course, travelled with Tom and me across the country on our thrift-shop and performance tours. As I've written, she also accompanied me, Tom, and Glenn Allison to Ottawa to install my ceramic murals, *Veneration of the White Collar Worker*. She had become not only my dearest friend but also an integral part of my creative team.

In the Kitsilano house, Tom was the only one of us with a TV, so we often retired to the basement after dinner to watch an old movie. We mostly sat on the floor. Friends dropped into that house too, during the evening. Again, there was much lively conversation and laughter. Around eight or nine o'clock, one of us would get up to make tea. Our friends stayed on and on, and I would be glad when they eventually left and I could go to bed. Elizabeth didn't mind how late it got; she was happy to stay up until the last dog was hung.

When I was about to be married, Tom and Elizabeth moved to "The White House" in Burnaby, which they shared with Jeremy Wilkins and Alfred and Elvira Siemens (who later took back her maiden name, Wiebe). There, I helped Elizabeth paint the sloping walls of her attic bedroom. She dressed it up with a wicker chair and beautifully patterned fabrics. Later, the whole group purchased a house together in Vancouver, on Prince Albert Street. Because of its green-shingled exterior, it was called The Green House. It was a place I dearly loved to visit.

In the late 1980s, after I moved to my newly built home in East Vancouver, Elizabeth came over often to help me start the garden and do some cleaning. Within eight months, she learned she had colon cancer. I was deeply afraid for her. She was convinced she would recover because, as she said, "Who would look after my dog?" Emma was a miniature poodle with a big brain, mischievous tendencies, and a stubborn streak. Seeing that the only person left at The Green House was Tom, and he was busy looking after his dying father, I suggested Elizabeth come to my house for her recovery. She did that. After two operations, about six months apart, the cancer was gone. However, her right hand and arm were paralyzed by an injury to a nerve during or after surgery. Her left hand and her feet were also slightly affected. At sixty-one, Elizabeth would not be able to do everything for herself anymore. She settled in permanently, taking the bedroom on the main floor. I moved into a newly built bedroom on the second floor.

Three years after Elizabeth's cancer surgery, I had an operation on my tailbone, which I had broken a few years earlier, falling on ice. The operation was a failure, leaving me in constant pain and unable to sit, stand, walk, or kneel for any extended period. The only time that the pain seems to remit is when I am working in my studio, absorbed in making art.

Elizabeth and I support each other in different ways, and here we still are, cooking, cleaning, enjoying visitors, entertaining our friends at summer teas and midwinter carolling parties. Elizabeth makes all of our bread and most of our other baked goodies. She also prepares many of our dinners. Her greatest claim to fame, however, is our enormous garden, which extends in healthy abundance from the boulevard in front of the house to the back lane. It is much admired by all who pass by and by those who come into the yard too. In summer, we have lunch or tea under the grape arbour, enjoying the cool breezes, the scent of the flowers, and the buzzing of the bees.

At St. Margaret's, the little Anglican church we now attend, we have shared many more good times and new friends. Elizabeth holds a position of honour there, having been awarded the Order of the Diocese of New Westminster for her unstinting work in the altar guild. She also makes all the communion bread for our church. In the meantime, I slink off to the studio to work on one thing or another.

In 2000, when I had my big retrospective exhibition at the Vancouver Art Gallery, I wrote this dedication for the catalogue: "To Elizabeth Klassen, whose nimble wits have seen things through from spectral and obscure intentions to solid live manifestations. I thank her for her cheers from the bleachers and her unstinted help when it was needed."

GIVEN HOW COMPATIBLE we are and how much we have done together, the art community long ago assumed that Elizabeth and I were lesbians. I remember remonstrating with the critic Joan Lowndes about it. She said, "Methinks the lady doth protest too much," then added, "It's all right, Gathie. We all love you." The repetition of that phrase by others was irksome to me. It seemed to miss the point. Now, both of us are used to being asked whether we are sisters. Elizabeth says no and I say yes. These things are not worth worrying about anymore.

Working on *Winter Tree* in my studio, 2012.

CANOES

AND

WINTER TREE

BY THE END OF 2007, I had finished a very dense installation called *Dreaming of Flying*. The title came from dreams I had had as a child. I was also thinking of moths, painted large. Not colourful and flamboyant butterflies with wings outspread, but plain moths with upright wings, seen from the side. But what to show with them? How to complete them? While visiting my brother Jack and his wife, Vera, in Sechelt, I saw their son's canoe stored upside down at the side of their house. That was it: moths and a canoe!

The moths were a joy to paint. The papier mâché canoe took me two years of struggle and frustration. Basically, I made it and took it apart in chunks, remade it and took it apart again, over and over. I didn't use an armature and it kept warping. There were problems with the different papers I used, in and under the paste, shrinking at different rates. Near the beginning of my canoe project, Pierre Théberge, then director of the National Gallery, visited my studio. He admired my idea. He came again about a year later when I was patching a rip in the side of the canoe. I used a bit of metal to bridge that gap and blundered on. My friends kept telling me to give it up. It wasn't working, they said. I was wasting my time. I ignored them.

Friends from church turned the canoe for me and also helped fill it with bags of pebbles to maintain its shape as it dried. On the outside, it was supported with bricks and wood. When it was finally whole, dry, and strong, I painted it off-white, with subtle and shadowy shifts of colour over the contours, from cool to warm white, and then I glazed it. Under bright lights, it looked almost iridescent. When I ran my hands over its surface, I thought of a bony old man. I installed the canoe, sitting on trestles, in the centre of the Equinox Gallery with mirrors hanging over it. The mirrors reflected the paintings of moths that were hung in gradations of colour, from dark to light, on the surrounding walls. Critics saw the canoe not only as a bruised and wrinkled old body but also as a large cocoon, from which the moths had recently emerged. Youth and old age. Life and death.

The National Gallery acquired *Dreaming of Flying* and displayed it in a pale grey room, the interior of the canoe flooded with light. It moved some viewers to tears. What better praise can there be? It was worth all the pain and the struggle.

Once I'd finished that first canoe, I was determined to make another. Perhaps this resolution was like getting back on the horse that has thrown you. This time I vowed it would be completed in two months, not two years. It took three months. Close enough. The second canoe was smaller and finished with aluminum paint; its appearance seemed to evoke a slice of silvery moonlight. I was happy with it, but no one was interested in showing it. It lay on top of the bookshelves on the second floor of my house for years, until Ellen van Eijnsbergen, the director of the Burnaby Art Gallery, asked to include it in an exhibition of my works on (and of) paper. At the time, I had been painting a picture of Elizabeth wearing a yellow ochre–coloured dress with tassels at the hem. In the painting, I extended the tassels, making them into ribbons. That's when I thought of draping the canoe in long ribbons of papier mâché painted mostly in rich colours. I called the work, simply, *Dressed Canoe.*

Also included in the *paperworks* show at the Burnaby Art Gallery in 2014 was an installation I'd just completed, which I called *Winter Tree with Leaves.* The idea for it came to me while I was on an afternoon walk around my neighbourhood. Mostly my walks take me down a number of streets to Trout Lake, in John Hendry Park. I always enjoy the trees on the way, in spring bud, in summer fullness, in the brilliant colours of fall. I also enjoy the fallen leaves which, by winter, are trod on, wet, mutilated. Earlier in the season, however, they retain their distinctive shapes, hues, and textures. I pick them up and take them home. There is an overflowing box of them in the studio.

Although both winter and summer trees intrigue me, I chose to make a winter tree. The papier mâché surface is uneven, with bumps, wrinkles, and protrusions. And I lopped off the ends of the long limbs and branches so that they looked like city trees, heavily pruned. (An engineer friend, Karl Brown, made metal supports so that I could remove the limbs to get the tree through a doorway.) I painted this pruned winter tree off-white, which was suggestive of—but not as obvious as—a birch. For the installation, I stood the tree in a small bed of dark gravel at the centre of the exhibition space, surrounded by big leaves in deep reds and browns and glowing yellows, painted on large sheets of paper. I left these paintings unframed and pinned them to the walls so that they could hang loosely. I wanted them to look as unprecious as possible. To complete the installation, I created a shadow of the tree in silver-painted paper and laid it across the floor.

To critics, the pale and slightly undulating surface of the tree once again suggested human flesh. And once again they saw recurring themes in my work: light and shadow, growth and decay, life and death—and rebirth.

MY FAITH,
OR MIRACLES
GREAT
AND SMALL

I AM A CHRISTIAN and an artist. I do not make Christian art—
just as the trees I have planted in my garden are not Christian
trees. They are trees. Still, when I started to paint seriously, in
the early 1960s, I thought I should depict ideas that I believed in
philosophically, things as they related to Christianity. I painted
some crucifixions, which people thought were about sex. That was
a total failure. I decided I would try to *be* Christian rather than
illustrate Christian teachings. If you have something serious to
say, you should be clear about it. If you paint it, it's not likely that
you will be very clear. You should write it or speak it. Better yet,
you should live it.

I have always believed in God and in Christ's teachings, but
definitely not all of any church's teaching. When I was a teenager, I was encouraged to read one chapter of the Bible every
day, and I did, and then read them again (although, after the first
time, skimming through all the "begats"). As I became an adult, I

A small Easter tableau in my house. Behind it is a
watercolour *fraktur*, a form of Germanic folk art,
that my friend Alfred Siemens made for me on my
fiftieth birthday. It includes lines from a sixteenth-
century prayer that was later set to music.

recognized that many of the stories in the Bible are expressed in metaphorical language, especially regarding our understanding of time and age. My beliefs sustain me. They are there like a solid fact that I can rely on. I spend a lot of time every day in prayer, for everybody and for everything.

My mother was a truly religious woman. She thought anyone who professed not to believe in God was just acting out, being naughty, pretending. In her world, there could be no one who did not believe in God. Mother's favourite activity was going to church, and when her children were young, she shepherded us there too. My brothers were not really interested and stopped attending in their teens. As a child, I found the service boring. What I loved was the singing, and I also enjoyed the funny stories, which lightened the sermons. Now I regret not having listened more closely to what was said.

Not surprisingly, my mother was worried about our religious upbringing, and when I was about nine, she initiated morning readings with Gordon and me. Jack had already left home. We always had a Mennonite calendar in our house, the kind you tear pages off each day. On the front of each page were the date and a short quote from the Bible. On the back of the page was a story based on the religious quote—a nicer story, I thought. Mother asked us to read these out loud after breakfast; I had to read the scripture, and Gordon was assigned the interesting story. After a while, he refused his part in our morning worship and I did both. The fact that these readings were in German, the only language my mother knew, did no harm to my broader education.

Evening prayers were entirely different. In our little home in Winnipeg, Mother and I slept in the living room and Gordon, in the small room off it. We all knelt in front of our beds at the same time. Mother's prayers came first, usually accompanied by tears. Gordon's prayers were his own. They were probably pretty good, but since I was farthest from him, with my back turned, I couldn't hear them. My prayers included serious matters. Shortly before the war, I had read about the German persecution of the Jews, something few people were talking about then. Later, I heard about the murders and disappearances of Russian Mennonites under Stalin. My mother and Gordon were not convinced that my praying would cause Hitler and Stalin to have a change of heart and action, but they didn't criticize me for it. Despite the accounts in the newspapers, I remained optimistic. Our nightly prayers were a warm and comforting part of our lives.

When I was young, I wanted very much to be a person of faith. Still, I couldn't see how I could get there while I was also so interested in movies and movie stars and other worldly things. It was like two different impulses fighting in me, and I worried about it a good deal. There was a point, however, when I was thirteen or fourteen, that I realized my faith was more important. I burned all my movie magazines.

All Mother's efforts to lead Jack and Gordon into the church came to nothing. When I was sixteen, however, I was baptized in a freshwater pool at Birds Hill, a former quarry outside Winnipeg. My mother was made very happy by my confession of faith, which included a testimony to her great efforts in educating us in Christ's teachings. Until then, others in the church had thought her a bad mother who failed to influence her children in their religious beliefs.

My own journey in understanding what the Bible and Christian teachings have to offer had just begun, and continues to this day. For many years, Elizabeth and I were members of the Killarney Park Mennonite Church in Vancouver. In the mid-1970s, after my marriage broke up, some close friends and I formed a house church, without sermons—we all felt we'd heard enough sermons to last a lifetime. We bought hymnals and a few music stands and worshipped in our own way, with prayers, Bible readings, other readings, and a lot of enthusiastic singing. Per-haps too enthusiastic for the neighbours. Elvira, Alfred, Jeremy, and Tom all sang beautifully, especially Tom in his classically trained bass-baritone voice. Elizabeth and I took the soprano parts. Jeremy and Elvira both played piano, and I had my violin restrung so that I could alternate between singing and playing. We discussed the scripture we had read with the knowledge that had accrued to us by then. After the service, we shared lunch or tea, exchanged stories, and talked about each other's problems and concerns. We very seldom had a formal communion service because we didn't feel it was necessary—our meetings and meals were themselves a fine kind of communion.

After our house church split up, Elizabeth and I attended the Point Grey Fellowship for a while. Now, however, because my back problems make any lengthy drive too painful, we go to a lit-tle Anglican church around the corner from our house. It offers us thorough teaching in a historical context and a contemporary one, fabulous prayers from the podium and the congregation, good singing, and, very importantly, a warm and generous commu-nity that works, eats, and enjoys being together. It is an inclusive church, which means that anyone may come and worship there.

ONE EASTER, ELIZABETH and I were on after-church tea duty, which necessitated a lot of baking. Because I have trouble stand-ing for any length of time, I couldn't take a very big part in the preparations, but Elizabeth, who is as old as I am, soldiered on through three consecutive days of work, early morning to late evening. She made Easter bread, or *pascha*, in all sizes, from large to small. She baked some loaves in empty tin cans and they looked like Russian architecture, bulging domes atop rounded towers. She also ran back and forth to the store for milk, cream, juice, fruit, cheese, and crackers. Then she was off to church to change the banners or the table linens and deliver the communion bread she had made. In the meantime, I made a couple of cookie sheets of squares. You can see who was and is the hero here.

On Easter morning, Elizabeth left the house early to get things in order. When I arrived, I helped with cutting and plating the food, finding cutlery, small jobs. Then we joyously attended the church service. A cross covered in ivy and fresh flowers was brought in by teenaged Ben and set in front of the altar by John. The Easter service seemed to be encapsulated in that bright, fresh cross, a symbol of Christ's death and resurrection. The readings, the prayers, the hymns, the sermon, the people—all were inspirational. With glad hearts and strong voices, we sang "Roll Away the Stone" and other hymns, new and old. Some of us went into overdrive, into a state that could be called ecstatic. We were celebrating the biggest, most important miracle in our lives.

Before the last hymn was sung, Elizabeth and I left the sanctuary and hurried downstairs. Our fellow parishioner Sandy was behind us, having assigned himself to assist us in our duties. We made tea and put everything on the big table. Sandy confiscated four pieces of Easter bread from a boy who had taken five of them. When everything was in its place, Sandy told us he would look after the kitchen and the table; we were to go out and enjoy ourselves. And we did. I got so engrossed in talking to friends that I failed to return to kitchen duty in a timely fashion. Elizabeth and Sandy had already done much clearing and cleaning. As we hurried to finish up, I expressed my gratitude to Sandy for his help. He said, "Helping is better than the alternative." What's the alternative, we asked. "The alternative is that you two stop making goodies." Then Sandy promised us he would always help us with church tea, and we knew we had fallen into the hands of a good Samaritan. Another miracle.

EPILOGUE

AS WITH MOST serious artists, I organize my weekday routine around time in my studio. I get up at eight o'clock, have a quick breakfast (toast, coffee, lemon water), and do the physical exercises that keep me fit and help me manage pain. Then I walk out the back door, across the courtyard that, in spring and summer, is lush with flowering trees and bushes—what joy!—and into my skylit studio. I work for a couple of hours and then return to the house to practise and play the piano for an hour. I play scales and studies followed by a few longer pieces I know well, mostly by Mozart and Beethoven. To keep my mind and fingers nimble, I also learn new works. After that, I eat lunch, and if there are no pressing appointments or meetings, I go back to the studio for another couple of hours.

My studio is brimming with work. In 2014, I began making abstract paintings, some of which appalled me. Eventually, I produced some large paintings that I really like. I recently completed and exhibited a series of paintings called *Water Again* that were a late-arriving sequel to *Pieces of Water*. I've been working on still-life paintings, too, for the Michael Gibson Gallery, my art dealer in London, Ontario. I'm also painting flowers, abstractly, for the Equinox Gallery in Vancouver. Also for the Equinox, I have made a new papier mâché dress that will be cast in a limited edition, not in bronze but in polymerized gypsum, a kind of sturdy plastic. These I will paint with acrylics. And I've taken on a commission for some people who bought a drawing I made in 1974 and who want me to make a painting of the same image.

This does not feel like the end of my story any more than it did a few years ago, in 2013, when I was awarded the Audain Prize for Lifetime Achievement in the Visual Arts. I told the audience at the awards ceremony that I hoped the honour did not suggest that my career was over. There certainly has been a lot of work in my life—a lot of work—and some people seemed to be saying, "Hang up your runners and rest. It's time to relax." But no, I told them, there's still too much to do: too many more things popping into my head, demanding to be seen. I wondered if there might be an After the Lifetime Achievement Award Award. And, perhaps, another award after that.

ACKNOWLEDGEMENTS

I AM THANKFUL for the enduring love and kindness of friends, family members, and fellow parishioners—many more than I could possibly name in this memoir. Particular thanks to Robin Laurence, who has made my art known far and wide and who has become a very good friend; Ann Rosenberg, who thinks my works are better than Picasso's; Scott and Corky McIntyre, who read my stories early on and believed in them; and Gordon Smith, who so generously supported my memoir project from the outset. I would also like to thank all the individuals and institutions that contributed photographs to the book, including Susan Falk, Tom Graff, Scott Massey, Richard Nelson, and the Vancouver Art Gallery. I extend appreciation, as well, to the Equinox Gallery, the Michael Gibson Gallery, and Pierre Théberge, former director of the National Gallery of Canada. —GATHIE FALK

I AM DEEPLY GRATEFUL to Gathie Falk for entrusting me with her memories, and to everyone at Figure 1 Publishing who invested so much care and expertise in the production of this book. Special thanks to Chris Labonté, Lara Smith, and Jessica Sullivan, who are all a joy to work with, and also to Lucy Kenward for her insightful and dedicated editing. —ROBIN LAURENCE

PHOTO CREDITS

Gallery, Acquisition Fund, VAG
86.31. Photo: Trevor Mills,
Vancouver Art Gallery.

*There are 21 Ships and 3
Warships in English Bay.*
Collection of the Vancouver
Art Gallery, Gift of the Artist,
VAG 2007.25.1 a-b. Photo:
Rachel Topham, Vancouver
Art Gallery.

*The Development of the Plot
III: #1 The Stage is Set.*
Collection of the National
Gallery of Canada. Photo:
Vancouver Art Gallery.

Dress with Insect Box.
Collection of the Vancouver
Art Gallery, Acquisition Fund,
VAG 98.63. Photo: Trevor
Mills, Vancouver Art Gallery.

Tom's Shirt I. Photo by Scott
Massey.

*Mostly Small Paintings: Fish
and Carrots.* Private Collection.
Photo: John C. Watts.

BLACK & WHITE FIGURES

Cataloguing data is available from Library and Archives Canada
ISBN 978-1-77327-012-8 (pbk.)
ISBN 978-1-77327-013-5 (ebook)
ISBN 978-1-77327-014-2 (pdf)

Design by Jessica Sullivan
Editing and proofreading by Lucy Kenward
Copy editing by Grace Yaginuma

Front cover: *14 Rotten Apples* (detail), 1970. Back cover: *30 Grapefruit* (detail), 1970. Collection of the Vancouver Art Gallery, Endowment Fund. Photos: Rachel Topham, Vancouver Art Gallery.

Inside front cover: *Low Clouds*, 1972, wood, paint, dimensions variable. Collection of the Vancouver Art Gallery, Gift of Peter Hendrie. Photo: Vancouver Art Gallery. Inside back cover: *Dressed Canoe*, 2008 and 2014, papier mâché, 317.5 × 45.7 × 35 cm. Photo: Scott Massey.

Printed and bound in China by C&C Offset Printing Co., Ltd.
Distributed in the U.S. by Publishers Group West

Every effort has been made to trace copyright holders and to obtain their permission for the use of copyright material. The publisher apologizes for any errors or omissions and would be grateful if notified of any corrections that should be incorporated in future reprints of this book.

Figure 1 Publishing Inc.
Vancouver BC Canada
www.figure1publishing.com

(overleaf) **Cement with Black Shadow**, 1983. Oil on canvas, 198.0 × 122.0 cm.
Cement with Poppies #5, 1983. Oil on canvas, 198.1 × 167.6 cm.

Theatre in B/W and Colour: Alberta Spruce & Streamers, 1984. Oil on canvas, 198.1 × 167.6 cm.

There are 21 Ships and 3 Warships in English Bay, 1990. Oil on canvas, wood, 234.0 × 152.3 cm.

The Development of the Plot III: #1 The Stage is Set, 1992. Oil on canvas, 228.6 × 160.0 cm.

Dress with Insect Box, 1998. Papier-mâché, acrylic paint, varnish, 90.0 × 60.0 × 55.0 cm.

Tom's Shirt I, 2016. Polymerized gypsum, acrylic paint, varnish, 76.2 × 73.7 × 17.8 cm.

Mostly Small Paintings: Fish and Carrots, 2016. Oil on canvas, 45.7 × 61 cm.